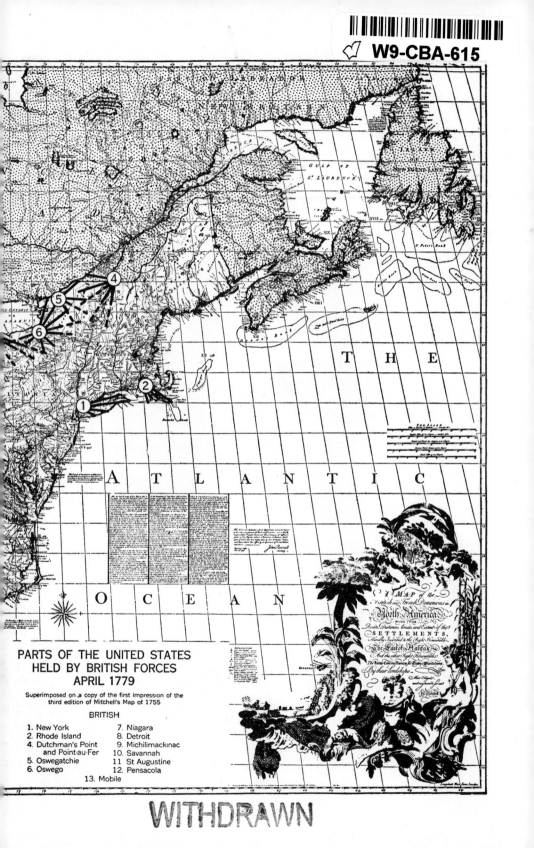

PARTS OF THE UNITED STATES
HELD BY BRITISH FORCES
APRIL 1779

Superimposed on a copy of the first impression of the
third edition of Mitchell's Map of 1755

BRITISH

1. New York
2. Rhode Island
4. Dutchman's Point
   and Point-au-Fer
5. Oswegatchie
6. Oswego
7. Niagara
8. Detroit
9. Michilimackinac
10. Savannah
11. St Augustine
12. Pensacola
13. Mobile

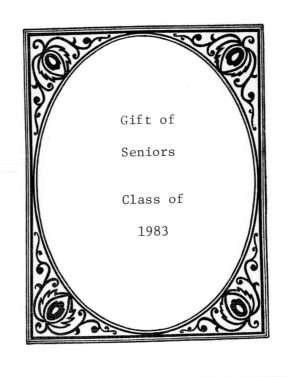

Gift of

Seniors

Class of

1983

THE HUSSEY-CUMBERLAND MISSION
AND AMERICAN INDEPENDENCE

THE
HUSSEY-CUMBERLAND MISSION
AND AMERICAN INDEPENDENCE

*An Essay in the Diplomacy
of the American Revolution*

BY

SAMUEL FLAGG BEMIS

COVER MAPS DESIGNED
FROM DATA FURNISHED BY THE AUTHOR

BY

COLONEL LAWRENCE MARTIN

*Chief of the Division of Maps
Library of Congress*

GLOUCESTER, MASS.

PETER SMITH

1968

PREFACE

I BELIEVE that the new source material from which this little volume is written gives a clearer understanding than has hitherto been possible of certain factors of European diplomacy one hundred and fifty years ago, and of their implications, through the connection of the Franco-American alliance, for American independence.

During a visit to Spain in 1928 I found, by the help of traces in W. R. Shepherd's *Guide,* a *legajo* of documents relating to the subject of this essay. The *legajo* has been used by the Spanish historian Dánvila y Collado,[1] but for rather general purposes and without the advantage of parallel English sources. The papers in the bundle were in utter disorder when I first saw them. I suppose this was because the encircling string may have broken in the hands of some careless *mozo* of the archives, letting the contents fall and scatter on the floor. In such cases *mozos* are likely to reassemble and tie up the papers as quickly and unobtrusively as possible, with no regard to original order. Señor Don Miguel Gomez del Campillo, then the accomplished chief of the *Sección de Estado* and now the Archivist of the *Archivo Histórico Nacional,* at Madrid, reduced the confusion of the documents to some order, and the entire lot was then photocopied by the Historical Mission of the Library of Congress. A few of the more significant pieces have been reproduced in the appendix of this volume. In the Public Record Office in London I

---

[1] *Reinado de Carlos III,* V, Chaps. ii, v. The *legajo* is also cited by François Rousseau, *Règne de Charles III d'Espagne, 1759-1788,* but the account of the Cumberland mission is neither complete nor reliable.

located Cumberland's confidential dispatches together
with his instructions and some other relevant matter.
The Historical Mission also made photostats of this
material. The Library of Congress already had a transcript of the manuscript memoir of Cumberland to Lord
Shelburne, in 1782, which has long been in the British
Museum[2] but apparently never used by Cumberland's
biographers. The papers of Lord George Germain, now
in the possession of Mr. William L. Clements, of Bay
City, Michigan, contain a volume of interesting Cumberland correspondence.[3] Mr. Clements kindly allowed
the Library of Congress to take photostats of these documents, which have been added to its collection of Cumberland material. For the French sources I have relied
on Doniol,[4] and on the Library of Congress transcripts
of the series *Correspondance Politique, Etats-Unis* in
the *Archives du Ministère des Affaires Etrangères*. The
American diplomatic correspondence, of course, has
long since been printed by Francis Wharton.[5] Less important material from the *Archivio di Stato* in Naples
and the *Archivio di Stato* in Venice was photocopied
by the Historical Mission of the Library of Congress.
I am indebted to Dr. Fritz Reinöhl of the *Haus-, Hof-
und Staatsarchiv* in Vienna for preparing the transcrip-
tion for me of Cumberland material found in the official correspondence of Prince Kaunitz with his sons,
successive Austrian diplomatic representatives at Madrid, one of whom was an intimate of Cumberland.

2 Additional MSS, No. 28851.

3 Calendared in *Stopford-Sackville Papers* (*Report of the Royal Historical Manuscripts Commission,* 1904, Vol. I). Citations in the text following
are to the manuscripts as indicated in the calendar.

4 *Histoire de la participation de la France à l'établissement des Etats-
Unis de l'Amérique* (Paris, 1890).

5 *Revolutionary Diplomatic Correspondence of the United States* (Washington, 1889).

A grant-in-aid from the American Council of Learned Societies assisted me in certain expenses connected with the assembling of material, travel within the United States, and the preparation of this manuscript. Miss Florence Spofford prepared the text of the documents which are printed in the appendix. Miss Grace Gardner Griffin assisted me with proofs.

Under the direction of its alert librarian, Dr. Herbert Putnam, the Library of Congress (aided by Mr. John D. Rockefeller, Jr.'s, contribution to the Gift Fund) has assembled hundreds of thousands of complete and well-indexed facsimiles of manuscript material in various archives of Europe dealing with American history. If the essay here presented be any contribution to the diplomatic history of the United States, I desire it to be testimony of the unrivalled possibilities of assistance, and of stimulation to endeavor, which are so intimately associated with that fine national institution and its able staff. I would particularly acknowledge the sympathetic interest and aid of Dr. H. E. Bourne, consultant in European history; Dr. M. A. DeWolfe Howe, consultant in biography; Dr. J. Franklin Jameson; Mr. C. K. Jones, assistant chief of the division of classification; and Colonel Lawrence Martin, chief of the division of maps.   S.F.B.

New London, N.H.,
August 26, 1931.

ABBREVIATIONS

AHN, *Est.* 4220, *Expdte.* 2, Doc. 99, means *Archivo Histórico Nacional* [Madrid], *Estado, legajo* number 4220, *Expediente* number 2, document 99 [or whatever other number the document cited may be].

R.O., S.P.F. means Public Record Office [London], State Papers, Foreign.

CONTENTS

CHAPTER I

To INTRODUCE the diplomatic episode which is to be the subject of this essay, we must recall the circumstances under which Spain entered the War of American Independence in 1779 as an ally of France but not of the United States. During the earlier years of that war the Spanish Government had joined France in furnishing secret aid in money and military supplies to the revolted American Colonies. This was not because of any sympathy for the republican cause, for, south of the Pyrenees, there was nothing at all resembling that exotic enthusiasm which animated French public opinion and supported the American policy of Louis XVI's Ministry. It must have been with some misgiving that Charles III's Government engaged in this business of secretly stimulating the rebellion of a people whom it refused to recognize politically, for might they not be setting a dangerous precedent for a monarchy whose position as a world power depended upon the tranquil and exclusive exploitation of its own extensive American colonies? Abetting rebellion, they were not eager for the world to know it, but they did want the strife in America to continue to the end that both English colonies and mother-country should be weakened as much as possible. Then at a favorable moment Spain might push her own interests to advantage.

That moment seemed to the Spanish Foreign Minister, Grimaldi, to be at hand in the summer of 1776, during the Portuguese crisis over the boundary question in the La Plata basin region, and he was ready to go to war with England at the side of France, if the latter monarchy would support Spain's intended conquest of Portugal. But the Comte de Vergennes, French Foreign Minister after 1774, though anxious enough to split apart the British Empire, hesitated to commit himself to a war from which Spain would draw the principal profits and thereby upset the balance of power in the Peninsula. When news arrived of the British victory at Long Island and the consequent occupation of the key position of New York City, these French hesitations crystallized into definite discouragement of Spanish readiness.

Then followed two years of watchful waiting on the part of France for decisive events in North America, accompanied by continued secret assistance to the American rebels in munitions and money. Thanks to this aid, and to the manifold blunders of the British War Office, presided over by Lord George Germain, the American forces were able to achieve the victory of Saratoga.

Saratoga caused a crisis in British politics. The North Ministry quickly resolved on a peace offer to the revolted Colonies—peace on the basis of self-government within the Empire and the repeal of the objectionable legislation passed by Parliament since 1763—and sent an official mission, headed by Lord Carlisle, to New York. The Carlisle peace commission was empowered to offer the Colonies all that they had demanded in 1775, and even more, but British sovereignty over them was to remain unimpaired.[1] Had that offer been accepted, the first and what might have proved to be the greatest

[1] The text of the instructions, appropriately annotated, is printed conveniently in S. E. Morison's documentary publication, *The American Revolution, 1764-1788*, 186-203.

of the self-governing commonwealths of an unimpaired British Empire would have taken root at Philadelphia, the seat of the Continental Congress. If the United States could have accepted in 1778 what would have contented the American Colonies only three years before, the history of the nineteenth and twentieth centuries would have been vastly different—it is not too exaggerated a conjecture that a Pax Britannica might be ruling the world today, and problems of the limitation of naval armaments would not be concerning British and American statesmen.

It is of particular interest to later phases of this study to note here that the Carlisle peace commission was empowered to recognize the *de facto* independence of the United States during the negotiations.[2] This was not intended as any real recognition of the independence of the United States except during the negotiation; the eventual treaty, to be embodied into an act of Parliament, was expected effectually to extinguish independence.[3]

It was exactly such a peace offer and possible reconciliation which France feared, when, after Burgoyne's capitulation, news reached Paris of the proposed British peace move. The French Ministry became more apprehensive when English emissaries appeared at the French capital and held confidential parleys with Benjamin Franklin and Silas Deane, the American envoys who, with Arthur Lee, for the year past had been im-

[2] ". . . We authorize you to admit of any claim or title to independency in any description of men, during the time of treaty, and for the purpose of treaty." Instructions to the Peace Commission of 1778.

[3] "As to the Declaration of Independence dated the 4th of July, 1776, and all votes, resolutions, and orders passed since the rupture began, it is not necessary to insist on a formal revocation of them, as such declaration, votes, orders and resolutions, not being legal acts, will be in effect rescinded by the conclusion of the treaty." *ibid.*

portuning the French Court to recognize the independence of the United States and to enter into an alliance. For Vergennes the time of watchful waiting ceased. With the Americans and British possibly on the eve of a reconciliation, he feared that the golden opportunity of breaking up the British Empire, of revenge for the prostration of France in 1763, might slip by forever. Without waiting to know definitely what Spain would do, Vergennes precipitately and without agreement with the Spanish Government, committed his king to a recognition of American independence and a promise of alliance. He took this hurried step in order to make sure that the Americans would not listen further to the allurements of British agents, and in order to be able to confront on American soil British formal offers of peace with the text of a treaty of recognition and alliance.[4] The actual signature of the Franco-American treaties, the one of amity and commerce, the other of alliance, was delayed until the 6th of February, 1778, in the vain hope that Spain might be induced to accede thereto. The alliance provided that if war between France and Great Britain should follow the former's recognition of the independence of the United States, the two allies should make common war and a common peace, either by truce or treaty, in which the recognition of American independence, absolute and unlimited as well in matters of commerce as of government, should be secured.

The Franco-American alliance arrived in America in time to counteract and to frustrate the proposals of the Carlisle commission for home-rule. Heartened by the victory of Saratoga, by the recognition of their independence by a great European monarchy, and by the new alliance and guaranty of that independence, the United

[4] *Am. Hist. Rev.*, XXIV, 474-496.

States firmly grasped the hand that France held forth across the ocean. The Continental Congress quickly ratified the treaty and promised not to make any separate peace or reconciliation with Great Britain. Defeated and dismayed, the English peace commission returned to London. The War for American Independence continued, as was the desire of France.

After the signing of the American alliance the primary purpose of French policy was to get Spain into that alliance, or at least into the war against Great Britain, and to line up the neutrals of Europe in combined opposition to British maritime policy. In the main Vergennes achieved this difficult task with matchless skill, and the resulting isolation of Great Britain was one of the factors which helped to win the war, much as one must emphasize the particularistic military efforts and diplomacy of Spain during the conflict. But for the Spanish alliance Vergennes had to pay a heavy price, for France's precipitate action in committing herself to the American alliance without adequate consultation with her family ally had been displeasing to Spain.[5] That monarchy had some time since settled her South American controversy with Portugal and had nothing to gain in that particular direction by war against England. Moreover it was a distinct slight to Spanish pride that an ally should have taken such a vitally important step independently, expecting Spain to follow as a matter of course. A different man had now taken the helm from the hands of the Genoese Grimaldi: Count Floridablanca, the ablest Spanish minister of his century, experienced, astute, disingenuous, patriotic, schooled in the sharp statecraft of that unscrupulous

[5] J. F. Yela Utrilla, *España ante la independencia de los Estados Unidos* (Lérida, 1925, 2nd ed.), 284.

age, a match for any of his contemporaries, who included
Vergennes, Kaunitz, Catherine II, and Frederick the
Great. He was resolved that Spain should not follow
blindly and implicitly in the wake of French policy, and
was determined that any move made on the part of his
government during this war was to be primarily for the
advantage of Spain. Before his king should agree to
enter the war, specific positive advantages must be set
down in black and white, and there must be a reasonable
certainty of getting them.

Any satisfactory adjustment of Anglo-Spanish affairs required for Spain the following: the restoration
of Gibraltar and Minorca; the retrocession of Florida;
the positive and permanent expulsion of British inter-
lopers from thé Bay of Honduras and the Campeche
Coast; and a share in the cod-fisheries of Newfoundland. These, and any incidental colonial conquests which
might be picked up from a defeated enemy, were the
objects of Spanish diplomacy; but the paramount object, the great thing that appealed to Spanish power
and pride, was Gibraltar. British possession of that
rock was a standing humiliation to Spain, even more
distressing than the British control of Dunkirk after
1763 was to France.

These objects might be secured from a successful war
against England, but Floridablanca first strove to win
without a war the fruits of one. By offering mediation
between Great Britain and France he suggested that
Spain might either maneuver Great Britain into an unsatisfactory peace, or might abandon her neutrality.
Such a move left to England the possibility of purchas-
ing at a high price the continuation of that neutrality.

In the Anglo-Spanish diplomatic conversations which
took place during the winter of 1778-1779 no specific

advantages for Spain were definitely stipulated, but there is no doubt what Floridablanca wanted. His diplomatic agents at London, Francisco Escarano, and the Marquis de Almodóvar, made that sufficiently plain to the British Ministry. Gibraltar was the price of Spanish neutrality. "They must know," wrote Floridablanca to Almodóvar, "that what we do not get by negotiation we shall know how to get with a big stick. Neutrality is a noose which they hold out to Your Excellency. Only when it is accompanied by specific positive offers with means of firmly guaranteeing them, can we begin to put any faith in it. . . . If that Court thinks we might be entitled to some favor, you already know the points on which this can be explained. Those Your Excellency has signified to them, the principal one being that pile of rock, Gibraltar, which is only a matter of expense and care to them, disturbing to us, an impediment to permanent friendship."[6]

George III would not offer Gibraltar nor anything else for Spanish neutrality. Floridablanca therefore dispatched an ultimatum of mediation to Great Britain and made a contingent alliance with the eager Vergennes, who was ready to agree to anything Spain might ask. The British Ambassador in Madrid received the ultimatum, April 3, 1779. The French alliance was signed April 12 (ratified at Versailles, April 28), 1779, before any answer could be received from England. The alliance, known as the convention of Aranjuez, stipulated that in case England should refuse the offer of mediation Spain would continue to fight until Gibraltar should be secured for Spain and until the French port of Dunkirk should be freed of its servitude or some acceptable equivalent rendered to the King of France. The con-

6 Dánvila y Collado, *Reinado de Carlos III* (Madrid, 1896), V, 10-38.

vention further listed, as desirabilities, the other minor objects of Spain. It is important to note here that each ally agreed not to make a separate peace, and not to engage directly or indirectly in separate peace negotiations.[7]

The terms of the Spanish ultimatum of mediation to the two belligerents are intimately connected with the negotiations that presently will engage our attention. Spain required a suspension of arms by France and Great Britain, of indefinite duration, not to be ruptured by either party except after one year's previous notice, and mutual disarmament. Both belligerents straightway were to send plenipotentiaries to a peace conference under the mediation of Spain, with Madrid suggested for the seat of the conference. At the mediation and intervention of the King of Spain, the King of Great Britain was to grant a suspension of arms to the "American Colonies," and to engage to the King of Spain to observe the terms of the suspension, promising not to break it without a year's notice in advance to the King of Spain in order that he might inform the same "American Colonies." In the Colonies a mutual disarmament similar to that between Great Britain and France should take place between Great Britain and the revolutionists. The boundaries of each of the "parties" were to be fixed on the basis of territory actually occupied by respective forces at the time of the suspension of arms, that is to say on the basis of the *uti possidetis*. "To settle these different objects and others relating to the solidity of the said suspension and the effects it is to produce while it lasts, one or more commissioners from the Colonies shall repair to Madrid, and His Britannic

[7] For English translation of text of the convention, see *The American Secretaries of State and their Diplomacy* (New York, 1927), I, 294.

Majesty will send his [plenipotentiaries] under the mediation of the King (if it be necessary) to settle the above articles, and during this time the Colonies are to be treated as independent in fact."[8]

Doubtless the presumptuous phraseology of this ultimatum was intended to prevent its acceptance by Great Britain, but as Professor Corwin has pointed out[9] so perspicaciously, it must have given Vergennes some anxious days. If the British Government had accepted, France would have been required either to accept or to reject the proffered mediation. If she accepted, it certainly would have been esteemed a violation of the Franco-American alliance, as Vergennes himself admitted,[10] for France could not ground arms and leave British troops in possession of New York and Philadelphia. If France rejected the mediation after Great Britain had accepted, it would have strained the Family Compact to the breaking point.

Fortunately for France and for American independence there was not the slightest danger that the British Ministry would accept. George III's Government refused to go to any peace conference which allowed a *de facto* independent status to the "American Colonies" even temporarily for the purpose of negotiating with them. We should remember, anent this Spanish offer of mediation, that recognition of independence *de facto* during and for the purpose of negotiation was no permanent recognition even of that limited status. The

[8] The text was printed in pamphlet form by the *Imprenta Real* of Madrid, 1779, a copy of which is to be found in the British Public Record Office, *State Papers Foreign*, Class 94, Vol. 254. This will hereafter be cited as R.O., S.P.F. For French translation of the essential parts, see Doniol, *op. cit.*, III, 850.

[9] *French Policy and the American Alliance* (Princeton, 1916), 215.

[10] Doniol, III, 801.

Carlisle commission itself had been instructed to allow the Colonies such a limited recognition merely during the negotiation, but the King of England would not now accept such a condition at the hands of a foreign mediator. Spain had worked too ambitiously, claiming Gibraltar and Minorca as rewards for the negotiation of peace; at least so the British Minister, Lord Weymouth, remarked to the Spanish Ambassador, when the latter formally withdrew the rejected offer of mediation.[11]

Almodóvar and his diplomatic staff crossed the Channel to Paris. Spain declared war, June 22, 1779. France was now bound by treaty to two allies, each the enemy of Great Britain. By the Franco-American treaty of February 6, 1778, neither party was to make peace with the enemy except jointly and then only when American independence had been secured, tacitly or explicitly, by truce or by treaty. The convention of Aranjuez required France to stay in the war until Spain secured Gibraltar. Was the United States, never an ally of Spain, bound through the obligations of its ally, France, not to make peace with Great Britain until that fortress should be relinquished to France's ally? Was the independence of the United States chained to the European Rock of Gibraltar by these diplomatic bonds of a secret Franco-Spanish alliance?

Spain entered the war expecting a quick and victorious campaign, thanks to the apparent superiority of the allied fleets[12] and the embarrassment of England with the American rebellion. As prearranged, the two allied fleets joined and cruised in the Channel to cover

11 Dánvila y Collado, op. cit., V, 55-59.

12 England had 123 fighting ships of one kind or another to France's 63 and Spain's 62. H. T. Colenbrander, De Patriottentijd (The Hague, 1897), I, 153.

the landing of a French army in England. Meanwhile Spain besieged Gibraltar and set in motion, from Havana and New Orleans, expeditions for the conquest and occupation of the Floridas and the expulsion of the British settlers from Honduras. In August of 1779 the family allies were patrolling the Channel with sixty-six ships-of-the-line as opposed to the British defensive fleet of forty sail, and 40,000 French troops at Havre and St. Malo awaited transports to England. There was real danger that a French army might soon deploy on English soil for the first time for over seven hundred years. It was not the preparations of the Government and country-folk to repel such an invasion but the inefficiency and unseamanlike qualities of her allied enemies which saved England. A sudden decision of the French to change their intended landing place from the Isle of Wight to the coast of Cornwall, and the rise of a fresh east wind upset the combinations of the joint fleet and unsettled the projects of invasion.[13] Eventually the whole enterprise, which had started under such promising circumstances, fell to pieces, and the fleets returned to their respective harbors. The plan for an invasion of England was abandoned, at least provisionally, and the allies planned another campaign, for the year 1780, of a less spectacular and decisive nature: to continue the blockade of Gibraltar, to keep a sufficient force in America and Asia to hold the British in check, and to assume the aggressive in the West Indies.[14]

The disappointing results of this campaign of 1779, on which Spain placed such great hopes may have been responsible for the secret discussions of peace which followed.

[13] A. T. Mahan, *Major Operations of the Navies in the War of American Independence*, 116-121.
[14] *ibid.*, 121.

CHAPTER II

WHEN the Spanish Ambassador quitted England, there remained in London the Abbé Thomas Hussey, chaplain of the embassy. He was a rebust and able Irishman born at Ballyboggan, County Meath, in 1741. Like many another Irish churchman he obtained his education in Spain, at the expense of the king of that country. Hussey received the degree of Doctor of Theology at the University of Seville, *Colegio de la Purísima Concepción*. After the completion of his studies in Seville he abjured the world of action and even of words and took the vows and commenced the severe discipline of the reformed Cistercian order, at La Trappe.

Immurement among the silent brethren of this austere and humble order must have ill become the active temperament of an athletic young man of colossal physical stature and equally generous intellectual endowment, including a genius for ecclesiastical and international politics. At any rate this particular priestly head was not to toss away the nights of many months on the scant straw-stuffed pillows of the dormitories of La Trappe. Hussey was destined, among other things, for the mitre, to preside in his later years over the Roman Catholic bishopric of Waterford and Lismore, and to be an energetic if uncertain factor in that rough and parlous chapter of Anglo-Irish history that preceded the Act of Union. At the Pope's mandate he left the Trappist monastery. He took holy orders. After a successful beginning of his secular career near the

Spanish Court, in Madrid, he became, about 1768, chaplain of the Spanish Embassy in London and eventually rector of the church associated with it. In the capacity of confessor he accompanied Prince Masserano, the Ambassador, then an ill man, home to Spain in 1778 and was with him when he died at Barcelona. In December, 1778, we find Hussey at the Spanish Court soliciting for an increase in pension, to be taken out of some Spanish see, that he might better be able to fulfil the worldly demands of his station in London.[1]

He was back in London before the summer of 1779, when he began duties as head of the Spanish intelligence service in England, availing himself of the lack of suspicion (so it was supposed) which would attach to the comings and goings of a "distinguished ecclesiastic, one of the Catholic leaders." At first he transmitted his reports to Paris,—whither Almodóvar the Spanish Ambassador had withdrawn,—through the agency of the Neapolitan Ambassador, Count Pignatelli. Despite the filial relationship which existed between the King of Naples and his father Charles III of Spain, Pignatelli soon received orders not to meddle with anything that might excite the suspicion of the

[1] Memorial of Thomas Hussey, undated, but answered at the Pardo, December 10, 1778. *Archivo de Simancas, Estado, legajo* 2363 *moderno.* He was granted 6000 *reales* expenses of travel to London and a pension of 500 to 600 ducats out of the proceeds of some bishopric to be designated for the purpose. [Floridablanca] to T. Hussey and to Don Miguel Muzquiz, Pardo, December 10, 1778, *ibid.* Presumably some delay occurred in finding the convenient bishopric to furnish the revenue, for Hussey had not begun to draw the increased pension in 1780, and it furnished him with an excuse to visit Spain in January of that year, for the purposes to be narrated in the text above.

The *Dictionary of National Biography* and the *Catholic Encyclopedia* have short accounts of Hussey's life, and both state that he was educated at the University of Salamanca. Hussey's memorial, however, specifically says Seville. The *Catholic Encyclopedia* gives his birth as 1746, the *Dictionary of National Biography* is authority for the date 1741.

Court of London. It then became necessary for Hussey
to establish another conveyance to Paris, and for this
purpose he visited the French capital in August, 1779.
He took along with him a *dossier* of official documents,
supposedly confidential, on the state of British naval
forces and the defenses of Gibraltar. These he procured
from one William Wardlaw, whom Hussey thought a
spy in Spanish pay, but who in reality was a British
secret service man, to whom the documents were furnished by Lord George Germain's knowledge and authority.[2] Therefore when Hussey returned to England
from Paris in the middle of September 1779, equipped
with a cipher and having arranged a channel of communication to Paris, he was known to the British Ministry as a Spanish spy. No steps were taken ostensibly
to restrain him and we may guess that much of the information which he continued to send to Madrid was
prepared for him discreetly by the British intelligence
service, then, as always, an effective and astutely conducted organization.

In some way, in November 1779, Hussey got into

[2] Almodóvar to Floridablanca, No. 223, Paris, August 23, 1779; Floridablanca to Almodóvar, S. Ildefonso, September 2, 1779, *Archivo de Simancas,
Estado,* 2364 *moderno (antiguo* 7005); Floridablanca to Aranda, S. Loren-
zo, Nov. 25, 1779, *Archivo Histórico Nacional, Estado, legajo* 4116. For
Wardlaw and the cognizance of Lord George Germain, see W. Wardlaw
to [Lord George Germain], and to [Richard Cumberland] June 8, and
August 9, 1779, in *Stopford-Sackville Papers* (Report of the *Royal Historical Manuscripts Commission,* 1904), Vol. I, 323, 324. Wardlaw in the
latter letter describes the information which Hussey asked for, and which
Wardlaw asked permission to sell "confidentially" to Hussey: description
of the general state of the navy, a plan of the new battery at Gibraltar,
with its subterranean magazine; statement of stores in the different naval
magazines; and a list of stores on board the ordnance ships going to the
Mediterranean. The letter of Almodóvar, No. 223, above cited, forwards
all this to Floridablanca, from Hussey, as very useful confidential information. See *Archivo de Simancas, Estado (Inglaterra) legajo* 2367 *moderno
(antiguo* 7005) for a *dossier* of additional information supplied by Hussey.

contact with Lord George Germain's *protégé*, Richard Cumberland, who was then serving as secretary of the Board of Trade. When Beaumarchais a few years previously had been in London "fixing" the strange affair of the Chevalier d'Eon and pursuing mysterious conversations with the American agent, Arthur Lee, he had posed as a buyer of old coin. So now Hussey stated that he had no other purpose in the capital than that of buying up mathematical instruments[3]—an explanation which deceived nobody. He then went on to suggest that the Spanish Court might be willing to consider a peace negotiation. Cumberland immediately laid the "proposal" before his chief, Lord George Germain, Secretary for War. Another conversation with Hussey followed. Cumberland assured him that "perfect credit was given him for the purity of his motives in the proposal he had made thro' my means." Then continuing with the views of Lord George Germain, but not the "concurrent sense of the King's Ministers," he said that Great Britain would herself welcome a discussion of peace, "and that if he (Mr. H.) would undertake a journey to Madrid for the voluntary purpose of bringing to this Court testimonials of the pacific disposition of Spain, I did presume it could not but be accepted by his Majesty's Ministers."

Hussey agreed to make the trip,—apparently his original "proposal" had suggested as much,—said that the ideas he had put forth were only his own personal views, avowed that he could exhibit no power from the Spanish Government. He asked to be fur-

[3] For further mention of this pretense see: Cumberland to Campo, Madrid, October 7, 1780, with endorsed reply; same to same, Madrid, October 24, 1780; and [Campo] to [Hussey], August 11, [1781], *Archivo Histórico Nacional, Estado* 4220, *Expediente* 2, Documents 184, 185, 191. This archive will henceforth be cited as AHN, *Est.* 4220, *Expdte.* 2, etc.

nished with powers from the British Government, any kind of powers which might serve the purpose of carefully distinguishing him for "what he really was, a disinterested mediator and not a [British] spy." He explained to Cumberland that a letter from Lord North, or Lord George Germain, might so serve, providing it were couched in such a way as not to appear that his trip was being undertaken as a result of Hussey's own proposal; this might "raise some suspicion or offense against him on the other side of the water, as being too forward and intrusive." After Cumberland objected that such a letter so written might be construed as a British solicitation to Spain for peace, Hussey agreed to leave the wording entirely to the minister. In all the negotiations that followed it was the effort of each party to avoid the appearance of itself beginning a negotiation. Each professed to be listening to a negotiation actually started by the other. We shall see that Hussey later represented the talk of peace to have been commenced by Germain.

In this conversation Hussey urged a prompt decision, for two reasons: Spain might soon make a treaty with France binding her not to make a separate peace; secondly, that he had secret information that Spain was on the point of sending an emissary to the American Congress. The conversation touched "at a distance" on possible peace terms. Hussey opined that Spain would demand Gibraltar as a *sine qua non* of any peace, but added "that he would not expose himself to the egregious folly of bringing to Great Britain a requisition of the cession of that important fortress, unless he brought ponderous equivalents in the opposite scale," and hinted that he had heard Spanish ministers say that they would offer a strong foothold on the Mosquito Coast, and another one at Oran on the Barbary Coast, and even perhaps an almost unlimited sum of money.[4] Hussey saw Germain, too, and had another conference with Cumberland, in which he appeared "inadvertently" to let slip an alleged quotation from the Spanish King to his Foreign Minister the previous August: "Floridablanca, we must have peace." According to the Abbé, Spain had no hopes of really capturing Gibraltar, and the war was unpopular with everybody except Aranda, the Spanish Ambassador at Paris. Despite Hussey's personal enthusiasm and the religious cast with which he tinctured it, Cumberland was convinced that these proposals and observations were made on instruction, and that the man could not be intending to desert his "trust" in England except he knew he was acting on the entire approval of his superiors. "He [Hussey] does not imply that a condition so very serious and humiliating to Great Britain as the cession of Gibraltar, can or ought to be entrusted and committed to him, but as he verily believes great and superior advantages would be offered by Spain for that fortress (as being the King's favorite object) he thinks it might be useful to Great Britain to know the Spanish propositions on that idea."[5]

If Hussey were acting carefully on instructions in thus putting forth, after the familiar manner of diplomatists, his personal ideas, I have found no evidence of it so far in the Spanish archives. Rather the representation which he made later to Floridablanca of these conversations, describing as British overtures what Cumberland had called Spanish proposals, and his general

[4] Cumberland to Germain, November 19, 1779, *Stopford-Sackville Papers*, I, 325-327.

[5] Cumberland to Germain, Queen Ann St., Saturday, November 20, 1779, 4 o'clock, enclosing heads of conversation with "Mr. H." *Stopford-Sackville Papers*, I, 327.

explanations in Spain, suggest that this whole peace imbroglio which was to follow may have had its original cerebral impulse in the fertile mind of the former Trappist monk. He had a long conference with Germain again on the 23rd of November. It was agreed that the priest should go to Spain. Germain furnished him with an autograph letter saying that if he observed any disposition for peace in Spain, "I can assure you, both for Lord North and myself, that your representations will be received with the most friendly attention; and if in pursuing the bent of your wishes you shall be warranted to convey to us any opening or overture on the part of Spain towards a pacification, so essential to the interests of both kingdoms, I can with equal truth assure you it will be entertained here with all possible sincerity and good faith."[6]

If the initiative in these conversations came from Hussey, there is on the other hand no doubt that the British Government was seeking an opportunity for separate peace parleys with Spain. Only two days after Germain's conversations with Hussey, Lord Hillsborough in a ministerial conference with Count Pignatelli, the Neapolitan Minister at the Court of London, suggested that the Crown would be infinitely glad to consider overtures of peace directly from "either" belligerent, "or promoted by any common friend whatsoever," providing they did not make the slightest mention of the rebellious Colonies directly or indirectly.[7]

---

[6] Lord George Germain to Mr. Hussey, November 29, 1779. It was acknowledged by Hussey, December 1, when he politely thanked Lords North and Germain for the good opinion of himself and the purity of his motives. *Stopford-Sackville Papers*, I, 329. The letter in Germain's own handwriting is in AHN, *Est.* 4220, *Expdte.* 2, Doc. 60.

[7] Pignatelli to Marchese della Sambuca, No. 817, London, December 3, 1779, *Archivio di Stato*, Naples, Series *Inghilterra Diversi*, 623, A 1779, Fasc. No. 33.

In the first mention of the subject Hillsborough professed to be speaking as a private individual, but he came back to it, without reservation, during the latter part of February 1780, suggesting that the King of Naples advise his father, Charles III of Spain, to make a separate peace.[8] This resulted in a non-committal response.[9] Subsequently strict injunctions to the new Neapolitan Minister forbade him to take any step in this business without first referring it back to the Court.[10]

Hussey reached Vittoria, December 24, 1779, presumably overland from France, and hastened a message ahead to Madrid, to explain to Floridablanca his sudden appearance in Spain, namely: that Lord George Germain, a secretary of state, and confidant of the British King, had revealed a disposition for a peace with Spain in which George III might not be unwilling to cede Gibraltar.[11]

[8] Same to same, No. 34, February 29, 1780, *ibid.*, A 1780, Fasc. No. 34.

[9] Instructions to Pignatelli, No. 846, Caserta, March 28, 1780, *ibid.* According to F. P. Renaut, *Le Pacte de Famille et l'Amérque* (Paris, 1922), 314, the King of Sicily sounded out his father, Charles III of Spain, who replied that he desired nothing less than an honorable peace compatible with the rights of his nation.

[10] Draft instructions to Principe di Caramanico [successor to Pignatelli], *ibid.* A 1780. This document is undated. Caramanico's first dispatch is dated London, May 25, 1781. Pignatelli's last dispatch is dated London, May 22, 1781.

[11] "On the 23rd of the last month I found myself with Lord George Germain, Secretary of State and the confidant of the King of Great Britain, interceding for the liberation of five priests who had been arrested for reasons of war. After having granted forthwith my affair, he began to say how sorry his Britannic Majesty was to find himself at war with Spain, and how keenly he would like to know the conditions which might move her to peace, and if they were not too hard the Court of London would accept them. He asked me if I thought the possession of Gibraltar would be a *sine qua non* for an accommodation, to which I replied that not having any confidential correspondence with the Court of Spain it was impossible for me to know its views and intentions. In all the rest of the conversation I kept myself entirely on the defensive, to see what would happen. He added that he did not believe his Britannic Majesty would find

The priest arrived at Madrid on the evening of January 3, 1780.[12] He saw Floridablanca either that night or the next day.[13] Following their conference Floridablanca drew up in his own hand the unsigned texts of reports for the chaplain to make to the British Ministry, as if it were Hussey's own words. After only a few days in the

so much difficulty as was thought in consenting to restore Gibraltar. George I had consented to the same, and even declared it in writing, and he (Lord George Germain) did not see that it was less practicable on this occasion.

"This conversation finished I went directly to see Count Pignatelli, the Envoy Extraordinary of the Court of His Sicilian Majesty at London, with whom I had orders to consult on such things as might turn up, who counselled me to inform you in cypher on the first occasion. But the next morning the subsecretary of His Britannic Majesty came to my house, told me that he was instructed about the conversation of the previous day; that Lord George Germain took up the subject with His Britannic Majesty; and that he had been ordered to find out from me if I would consent to go to Madrid in order to make known there the desires and intentions of the Court of London. I told him that I would think it over and make him a reply the following day. I returned to see Count Pignatelli, who told me he did not see that any harm could come from making such a trip, that perhaps Your Excellency could make use of it for divers purposes of which he and I were ignorant, that it would be convenient to the royal service to accept it and to start me on my journey right away. All the rest which the Secretary of State communicated to me orally and in writing would be too much to trouble you with in this letter, but I will give you a faithful account of it when I have permission to present myself personally, since I was asked by the Court of London not to communicate except directly and in my own person, a permission which I crave upon arriving at Madrid, which will be, God willing, within a week.

"I confess I enjoy very little ease, until I know whether I was right in undertaking this trip and thus have merited the approbation of Your Excellency. Anyway, even though I may have made a mistake I hope Your Excellency's kind heart will condescend to pardon my lack of experience and will trust the rectitude of my intention which certainly has no other object than to serve His Majesty with all the zeal of a faithful vassal and to obey altogether the orders of Your Excellency, whose hands I kiss,

"Your most devoted servant and Chaplain."

AHN, *Est.* 4220, *Expdte.* 2, Doc. 61. A search of Count Pignatelli's dispatches in the *Archivio di Stato* in Naples revealed no trace of these particular conversations with Hussey.

[12] Hussey to Floridablanca, Madrid, January 3, 1780, AHN, *Est.* 4220, *Expdte.* 2, Doc. 66.

[13] Floridablanca to Hussey, Madrid, January 4, 1780, *ibid.*, Doc. 76.

Spanish capital the pious agent hurried back to London in the guise of an ecclesiastic commissioned to arrange for the exchange of prisoners, with an ostensible letter of recommendation on that score to Aranda in Paris (to whom of course he needed no introduction of any kind), and a message of thanks to Count Pignatelli for the kind attention shown. He was already back in London by the 31st of January. He straightway delivered to Germain the remarks which he had received from Floridablanca. These were originally drawn up in two sets of memoranda. One had been entitled by the Spanish Minister, "What I was able to discover and ascertain when treating with the Ministry under the pretext of putting into effect an ecclesiastical pension which was awarded to me two years ago." It was to this effect: if England would surrender Gibraltar under the guise of being starved out, Spain would grant an honorable capitulation, paying the money value of the military stores, as assessed by a mixed commission, and releasing the British troops for service in other theaters of warfare, either in the "British Islands" or in the American Colonies; and the King of Spain would further promise not to make any engagement with the American Colonies, and to refrain from insisting to France on carrying out plans for an invasion of England. A mutual agreement to abstain from conquests in each other's colonial dominions might also be possible. Although the King of Spain would never consent to desert his ally, still if some formula could be found which would honorably fulfil the pledged word to France—pledged, thanks to the careless and extravagant action of the former [Spanish] Ministry two years ago—he would take it upon himself to indicate to France and to the Colonies a plan of accommodation which would keep the latter dependent in some way on the mother country, to achieve which end a few points might be conceded. Above all, haste was needed. Everything depended upon an agreement being reached before the end of February; for Mr. Jay,[14] recently President of Congress, was even now on his way to the Spanish Court, and once any Spanish engagements were entered into with the American Colonies it would be too late to consider a peace negotiation. Again, secrecy, entire and absolute secrecy was necessary.[15]

That is to say, Floridablanca, carefully concealing his own authorship of this secret report, putting it into the mouth of the priest Hussey in order to avoid any French accusations of Spanish disloyal separate peace moves in case the document should be discovered, suggested that if Great Britain would give up Gibraltar Spain would cease to prosecute the war energetically and would put pressure on France to accept a peace by which the American Colonies would continue dependent on Great Britain. This suggestion was backed up by some pretty direct and important intimations in a second memorandum, also written by Floridablanca and put over into the Abbé's handwriting as a confidential report by himself. The second memorandum was based

[14] John Jay and his secretary, William Carmichael, had landed at Cadiz, January 22, 1780. Carmichael, with an advance message for the Spanish Court, left Cadiz for Madrid, in company with the returning French Minister to the United States, on January 27, 1780. They arrived at Madrid, the night of February 11, 1780. Jay did not reach Madrid till April 4, 1780. Wharton, *Revolutionary Diplomatic Correspondence of the United States,* III, 470, 710.

[15] AHN, *Est.* 4220, *Expdte.* 2, Doc. 70. There are three copies of this document: a first draft in Floridablanca's hand, unsigned; a fair copy; and a third copy in Hussey's hand, unsigned. For text see Appendix No. 1. A letter embodying the sense of this was sent to Germain by Hussey, via Lisbon, January 8, 1780, from Madrid, just before he departed for London. *Stopford-Sackville Papers,* I, 329.

on the existence of some further, separate English overtures for peace which had just reached the Spanish Minister from another source, overtures which were more
specific and more alluring, but less direct and responsible than those which had come through Hussey. These
must now be examined before we pursue Hussey's further conversations in London, and note the Spanish
Minister's reaction to them.[16]

16 There is some other evidence to suggest that Floridablanca was searching for peace in January 1780, for on the 28th of that month he instructed
P. Normande, the Spanish chargé at St. Petersburg, to welcome casually
on his own responsibility, a Russian mediation, if a suitable opportunity
should present itself; and he prepared in February, 1780, to replace Normande with a more important personage, the Marques de la Torre. The
spoliations issue with Russia, which precipitated Catherine's Declaration of
Armed Neutrality of February 28, 1780, intervened to frustrate this. Dánvila, V, 339-343.

CHAPTER III

THE JOHNSTONE OVERTURES

WHEN Floridablanca prepared the data to be exhibited by Hussey in London he had some further reason than the Abbé's opinions to believe that the British Ministry might be considering seriously the purchase of a separate peace with Spain by the cession of Gibraltar. Overtures to that effect, purporting to have the sanction of Lord North, had reached him from Lisbon. Commodore George Johnstone, notorious British naval officer and pistol-fighter, former governor of the colony of West Florida, more recently member of Parliament, in which capacity he had played an egregious rôle in the unsuccessful negotiations in New York and Philadelphia of the Carlisle peace commission of 1778, was now in command of a British naval squadron on the Portuguese station.[1] While his ships were refreshing in the Tagus, Johnstone spent much time on shore, and characteristically, talked a great deal. He held converse with one Luis Cantofer,[2] a Portuguese trader who enjoyed the acquaintance of Floridablanca. Cantofer says Johnstone asserted that he had just had some conferences with Lord North before leaving London; and that the British King, as well as the Prime Minister, desired a secret understanding with Spain, for which England

[1] *Dictionary of National Biography.* Johnstone's official title was "Commodore and Commander-in-Chief of His Majesty's Ships and Vessels Employed and to be employed from Cape Finisterre to Cape S. Vincent and along the Southern Coast of Portugal," according to the volume of his official naval correspondence in Record Office, Admiralty, Series I, Vol. 387, which volume contains no allusions to the proposals above considered.

[2] The name occasionally appears as Louis Cantoferd.

was willing to make these sacrifices: for the neutrality of Spain, Gibraltar; for a Spanish alliance to help subjugate the revolted American Colonies of Great Britain, Florida and the fisheries of the Grand Banks of Newfoundland would be added to Gibraltar. Johnstone even wrote out a letter of introduction for Cantofer to present to Lord North in London, if he could get Floridablanca to commission him as a secret emissary on such an interesting business, and Cantofer went so far as to offer his services.

The Johnstone proposal and Cantofer's statements thereon, were speedily transmitted to Floridablanca, through the Spanish Ambassador at Lisbon, Count Fernan Nuñez. Orally Johnstone had laid down to Cantofer, who wrote them out, the following "articles of preliminary conditions to serve as a basis for negotiations":

"The city and fortress of Gibraltar with all its dependencies will be surrendered to His Catholic Majesty as soon as the articles agreed upon between the two Courts shall be executed.

"His Catholic Majesty will pay to His Britannic Majesty the total value of munitions, artillery, and other military supplies found at Gibraltar at the time of delivery, by means of a just appraisal to be made by commissioners appointed by both parties.

"His Catholic Majesty will maintain a perfect neutrality, closing all his ports to American vessels, throughout the duration of the war between England and her revolted Colonies of North America.

"If His Catholic Majesty should desire to join his forces to those of His Britannic Majesty to subjugate the revolted Colonies of North America and restore them to a dependency on their mother country, His Britannic Majesty will cede to His Catholic Majesty Florida and the cod-fisheries of the Banks of Newfoundland.

"Such, Sir, are approximately what Mr. Johnstone thought might be the basis of the negotiation. As to other articles on the part of Spain, of which mention was made in the last manifesto [anent the declaration of war], the Court of London would be pleased to make just satisfaction to His Catholic Majesty."[3]

Floridablanca's first use of the Cantofer letter was to send it to the French Court. He emphasized this gesture of loyalty with a copy of his own reply to the Portuguese merchant.[4]

At Versailles the correspondence was received with appropriate feeling as an expression of loyalty befitting the circumstances.[5] But Floridablanca, though suspici-

[3] Louis Cantoferd à S. E. Monsieur le Comte de Floridablanche, Lisbon, November 30, 1779, enclosed in covering dispatch of Fernan Nuñez to Floridablanca, November 30, 1779, AHN, *Est.* 4220, *Expdte.* 2, Doc. 3. We have given an English translation of Cantofer's French. See also Johnstone to Lord North, Lisbon, November 30, 1779, which is the letter of introduction for Cantofer, *ibid.*, Doc. 30.

[4] "Informed of what you write me the King my Master orders me to state to you that His Majesty's delicacy as to points of honor would make him hear and answer with the most burning indignation to such propositions if the emissary had not taken the respectable name of His Britannic Majesty. The King finds no object of interest in this world which could separate him from the engagements contracted with his most Christian nephew and ally, nor cause him to abandon a part which the conduct of the British Cabinet has caused him to take. Nor does His Majesty see in the Commodore any signs of authority to treat on subjects of such importance; and any negotiation to be commenced ought to be formal, honorable, and in good faith, so that it might be communicated to the belligerent powers." Campo's draft of Floridablanca to Cantofer, Madrid, December 10, 1779, *ibid.*, Doc. 5.

[5] [Floridablanca] to Aranda, Aranjuez, December 13, 1779, remitting original of Cantofer's letter, and copy of Floridablanca's reply, *ibid.*, Doc.

ous of Johnstone's character and lack of powers and unwilling to give hostages to fortune by sending any Spanish emissary to England as Johnstone had proposed, nevertheless kept open, through Nuñez and Cantofer, this covert communication with the English naval officer, being careful to profess the while that the King would not sell his neutrality for so much, like a pound of pears,—an old phrase which Floridablanca had used while trying to sell Spanish neutrality for Gibraltar to England the year before,—and that no negotiation would ever be possible except through regular and decorous channels, more proper than the discredited "schemer" Johnstone. No copy of this letter[6] was displayed to the French Court, nor of the further reports of Nuñez and Cantofer on conversations with Johnstone which continued, off and on, until the next May.[7]

6; Louis XVI to Charles III, December 25, 1779, Doniol, IV, 448, note 2; and Vergennes to Montmorin, December 24, 1779, *ibid.*, 475.

[6] "Your Excellency will please read the enclosed letter and deliver it to Cantofer. This Johnstone is a discredited schemer capable only of introducing quarrels and divisions, as he tried to do in the Colonies. He insults the King in proposing that he sell his neutrality like a pound of pears and abandon his engagements and friends, after His Majesty has been obliged, because of rebuffs and offenses, to have recourse to war. If the propositions should have proceeded to the question of His Majesty's speaking with his ally to reach a rational settlement they would have had another aspect, even at this late day; but the negotiation would have to be conducted through channels more free from all suspicion than Johnstone. France will not yield on the point of the independence of the Colonies; yet there should be some way of reconciling this with English honor if the British Ministry, trusting to a gift of fortune which is not one of those of the Holy Spirit, does not let the right moment slip by. Your Excellency may explain things in this way to Cantofer, endeavoring to find out if the English have made some overture to France, thus trying to carry water on both shoulders at the same time (*para mascar a dos carillos*), deceiving us as usual with their trickery. I suppose probably all this will be useless to you once that Johnstone has departed leaving behind him such an extraordinary rocket as that. Your letter about the Annobon matter has arrived and will be answered." Confidencial del Gefe [Floridablanca] al Conde de Fernan Nuñez, December 10, 1779, AHN, *Est.* 4220, *Expdte.* 2, Doc. 4.

[7] AHN, *Est.* 4220, *Expdte.* 2, Docs. 27, 28, 29, 32, 34, 35.

We have said that the subject matter of these proposals of Johnstone is closely connected with the second memorandum which Hussey carried back to London early in January 1780. Like the first set of observations, Floridablanca wrote this out carefully in his own hand, with studied corrections, and the ecclesiastic copied it.[8] The Spanish Minister had the audacity, or perhaps the sense of humor, to prepare this second series of observations as if written by a British agent, with the title, "Confidential: Notes on Matters that I have ascertained, and other things that occur to me *for my government (para mi gobierno)*." They mentioned the Johnstone overtures, said that Spain would not send an agent to England for fear of exposing herself to France, advised the immediate evacuation of Gibraltar in order to gain the full confidence of Spain and to prevent that nation from making an alliance with the American Colonies and lending herself to an immediate invasion of England, and suggested that if this were done Spain could immediately be placed in a "most useful kind of neutrality"; further, that the King of Spain would intervene to induce France to join a peace by which Great Britain would grant the "Colonies" a "vague feudal dependence like the free cities of the Empire." It was suggested that the details of all this might even be settled with Mr. Jay; the Colonies would be restricted in their independence by some softening of their "yoke of subjection."[9]

These memoranda of Floridablanca, together with certain other of that Minister's confidential communica-

---

[8] Though not dated, the close relationship of this memorandum to the Johnstone proposals indicates that it was written at the time of Hussey's January visit to Madrid.

[9] For text, see Appendix No. 2.

tions about to be examined, again emphasize the real objectives of Spanish policy in the War of American Independence: to recover Gibraltar and Minorca, and then end the war as quickly as possible, picking up at the peace any incidental advantages, such as Florida, the codfish fisheries, and regulation of the question of the woodcutters of Honduras. Gibraltar secured, peace could be had by pressing France with some casuistical formula construed out of a strained interpretation of *tacit* independence for the American "Colonies." This would be represented as fulfilling the letter of the obligations of Article VIII[10] of the Franco-American alliance, that fateful alliance to which Vergennes had committed France without consulting Spain. Could Vergennes, who had taken that momentous step on French responsibility alone, fairly object now if Spain, having satisfied her principal war aims, should shrink from throwing her whole energy into the continuation of a war to enable France to wring from Great Britain an explicit recognition of the unqualified independence of the United States? Hooked to such an unwilling Spanish ally, Vergennes might find it practical to patch up a peace without any *de jure* recognition of American independence, taking refuge in the ambiguities of Article VIII. Already Floridablanca in his diplomacy of the previous year had held forth Spanish neutrality for Gibraltar. Already he had offered in vain Spanish mediation upon the basis of *de facto* independence,—*during* the negotiation,—for the American "Colonies," on the basis of *uti possidetis,* which would have left in the pos-

10 "Article VIII. Neither of the two parties shall conclude truce or peace with Great Britain, without the formal consent of the other first obtained; and they mutually engage not to lay down their arms until the independence of the United States shall have been formally or tacitly assured by the treaty or treaties which shall terminate the war."

session of Great Britain, New York, Long Island, Rhode Island, and the northern frontier. Already Vergennes had once awaited in suspense the answer of the British Ministry, for an acceptance by George III of the Spanish mediation would have destroyed the Family Compact or the Franco-American alliance, one or the other. Already the obstinacy of George III and the North Government had saved Vergennes from this terrible choice. Could he rely on such blindness of his enemy again? Or would the calamities of war and the posture of European diplomacy now induce Great Britain to pay for peace with Spain what she would not pay in 1778-1779? Would Lord North's Ministry be really frightened by Jay's appearance in Spain and the empty threat of an alliance with him? Or disturbed, after the allied naval fiasco of 1779, by Spanish threats of an invasion of England?

On the answer to these questions hung once more the fate of American independence. Meanwhile the United States, ignorant of the real significance of the impending negotiation, remained oblivious to the danger of Hussey. It was left for Vergennes, when he eventually discovered what was going on, to bear the burden of worry and the strain of conscience imposed by Floridablanca's tortuous diplomacy. It remains for the twentieth century student to see how these negotiations entangled the cause of American independence with the subtle and secret diplomacy of France's family ally.

Bearing these Spanish messages, Hussey reached London at the end of January and conveyed to Lord George Germain the ideas of Floridablanca. He urged him to hurry back a reply before Mr. Jay should reach Madrid, even though, as he explained, thanks to his own intercession, Floridablanca had been prevailed upon to engage solemnly his word that nothing would be concluded with the American envoy, "nor even a promise given him of alliance with the British Colonies," until the answer of the British Ministry should reach Madrid. That is, provided it came by the end of February. No "affected delays" would be tolerated. Not only haste was necessary, but secrecy, absolute secrecy. In Spain the only persons who knew of this business of peace were the King, the Prince of Asturias, Floridablanca, and the latter's secretary, Bernardo del Campo.[11]

One of Hussey's weaknesses as a secret diplomatist or ecclesiastical go-between, or intelligence agent, or chaplain, or confessor, or whatever he was, was his propensity for inserting an idea of his own into a professedly objective representation. Possibly it had been Floridablanca's purpose to guard against this when he took the care to write out himself exactly what he wanted Hussey to say to the British Ministry. These Spanish memoranda nowhere include one of the statements that Hussey actually made to Germain; that His Catholic Majesty remained *"not in the least tied down to any articles* which may prevent him from coming into a *separate* and honorable accommodation with Great Britain."* This was—next to Spain's insistence on Gibraltar—the most significant statement which Hussey made to the British authorities.

One thing the Abbé learned immediately in London. The Johnstone overtures were without any authority. The Ministry completely disavowed them. This must have been a matter of chagrin to Floridablanca; but at least it threw Johnstone out of the running as an intermediary and left Hussey alone in that not unwelcome

[11] Hussey to Germain, Richmond Bldgs., January 31, 1780, AHN, *Est.* 4220, *Expdte.* 2, Doc. 79.

rôle. He professed to be pleased to hear this, and said that it would please the Spanish Court.[12]

Though the British Ministry did not respond with the desired alacrity to the priest's impatient importunities,[13] a reply was vouchsafed with reasonable promptness. Hussey rushed it to Spain in a cipher dispatch dated London, February 16, 1780, and carried by one of his personal servants who bore a passport signed by Lord Stormont:[14]

"When I arrived here about two weeks ago I conveyed to this Cabinet what Your Excellency told me to. They considered the subject tenaciously for several consecutive days, but they could not agree to bind themselves to the evacuation of Gibraltar as a first and indispensable article of the negotiation. The Government offers to treat with Spain on the basis of the treaty of Paris; and then if in the course of the negotiation Spain wants to treat on the subject under the caption of an exchange of territories, Great Britain will enter into the matter and says that the world will finally see how sincerely she desires peace with Spain. In case Your Excellency should judge this a sufficient beginning for a treaty, Great Britain will appoint a confidential person to undertake the negotiation promptly and secretly with a similar person on the part of Spain and if Your Excellency will permit me the conjecture, I think that the evacuation of Gibraltar will enter into the negotiation, but I

12 Hussey to Lord George Germain, February 3, 1780, *Stopford-Sackville Papers,* I, 331.

13 In his letter to Germain, February 3, 1780, he urged it before the next mail. *Stopford-Sackville Papers,* I, 331.

14 Then Secretary of State for the Northern Department.

do not have any authority by word of mouth or in writing from the English Government to support this. This Ministry declares that it has given no commission nor instructions to Johnstone regarding the proposals made at Lisbon; and says that accordingly it hopes the latter's impudence will not serve to obstruct these negotiations."[15]

On the one hand, in his reports to the British Ministry, Hussey had gratuitously represented the King of Spain as not tied down to any articles with France that would prevent a separate treaty between Spain and Great Britain. Now he was representing to Floridablanca his own unsupported opinion that Gibraltar could be had in such a separate peace negotiation, and weaving that opinion into a letter which represented the British Government as willing to make this surrender in some sort of secret articles of exchange to be signed at the same time as a public treaty of peace. These representations are doubtless responsible for much of what was to follow, for they led each government to believe that there was a chance of achieving its principal object: England hoped for a separate peace, Spain for Gibraltar.

Recent military events made such a negotiation more attractive to Spain. If the failure of the allied fleet operations during the previous summer had been dis-

---

[15] AHN, *Est.* 4220, *Expdte.* 2, Doc. 82. In an *open* covering letter Hussey says he is sending the cipher dispatch by special messenger at the request of the British Government *"in order not entirely to close the door to the proposal in the* [ciphered] *letter,* for here they are very confident that a reply will be returned consenting to the proposal. In order not to be responsible to God for the consequences, I myself do not dare to say what will result, but I am sorry that they have not opened up more here in regard to the *principal point. ibid.* The special messenger was Hussey's own servant, presumably one Daly, who plays such a part in later negotiations. *ibid.,* Docs. 93, 26.

couraging, the military ardor of the Spanish Ministry must have been further dampened by Sir George Rodney's defeat of Admiral Langara's Spanish squadron off Cape St. Vincent, January 7, 1780. Only four of Langara's eleven ships-of-the-line escaped, and of the remaining seven Rodney brought four into Gibraltar and added them to the British fleet. This heavy blow relieved the sorely beleaguered garrison there and was followed by the provisioning of Minorca before the English fleet, according to concerted campaign plans, departed for the West Indies, again leaving Gibraltar to defend itself.[16] Men were thinking of the relief of Gibraltar and of the consequent postponement of a victorious Spanish peace when Hussey's cipher dispatch of February 16, 1780, above quoted, reached Madrid, suggesting that the British Ministry, to secure peace with Spain, perhaps might hand over the fortress which Rodney had so gallantly relieved.

On receipt of Hussey's message Floridablanca immediately summoned a special council of ministers on the evening of the 28th of February, 1780. Lucidly he recapitulated in detail the history of the negotiation, representing it as having come at the instance of England, proposed to Spain "individually." He stated that now was the moment for a "quick and critical decision" as to whether to appoint a plenipotentiary to treat for peace with an authorized British agent. He asked for brief opinions in writing from each minister, on three particular points:

1. Should the Spanish Ministry enter into peace discussions with the British Ministry, or reject the proposals which had been made to that end?

[16] A. T. Mahan, *Major Operations of the Navies in the War of American Independence*, 120-125.

2. In case the negotiations were commenced should the fact be communicated to France?

3. In case it were not best now to communicate the fact to the French Court, when should it be communicated?

There is no evidence that Floridablanca quoted to the Ministers the text of article III of the secret convention of Aranjuez, by which Spain had agreed not to treat separately, directly or indirectly, with the enemy.[17]

Four ministers participated in the deliberations in addition to Floridablanca, and each handed in a written opinion, all dated February 29, 1780: Josef de Galvez, Minister for the Indies, Count Ricla, Minister for War, the Marquis Gonzales de Castejon, Minister for the Navy, and one other, evidently Muzquiz, Minister of Finances, whose opinion is not signed. All four separate written opinions agreed that the negotiation should be commenced, secretly and separately, with England, without apprising France. On the third question, Galvez and Ricla thought that nothing should be communicated to France until a definite agreement had been reached with England; the other two answers were vague on this point. No minister presumed to advise as to the terms of peace—this was left to Floridablanca as peculiar to his own province. The several answers and the labored justification for eluding the obligations of the French alliance are worth reading in their entire text.[18]

[17] "Their Catholic and Very Christian Majesties renew the obligation of Article XVII of the Family Compact, and in consequence thereof promise not to listen to any direct or indirect proposal on the part of the common enemy without communicating it each to the other; and that neither of the two Majesties will sign with the said enemy a treaty, convention or any act of whatsoever nature without the knowledge and previous consent of the other."

[18] Cabinet opinions as to proposed secret peace negotiations with Eng-

"At the same time" of the arrival of Hussey's London dispatch of February 16, some further interesting proposals from the disavowed Johnstone reached Madrid. Hussey's dispatch, which had caused the sudden council meeting of February 28, had passed through Vittoria on February 24, the same day that Fernan Nuñez forwarded from Cantofer some new peace articles, concocted by Johnstone, who had been again in port and on shore, and had talked unreservedly even at the dinner table about the anxiety of Great Britain to make peace with Spain by yielding Gibraltar. He professed to Cantofer that he had received new instructions from Lord North.[19]

Although the new Johnstone proposals are mentioned on March 2, 1780, by Floridablanca as having been received "at the same time" as Hussey's dispatch of February 16, we cannot say whether they were received before or after the council meeting of the evening of February 28. It is not likely that they were expounded by Floridablanca that night, if only because it took about five days for a courier to reach Madrid from Lisbon.[20] As he read this Lisbon dispatch, Floridablanca knew that the man Johnstone now had no credit. Nevertheless the new Johnstone articles played an important part in the formulation of Floridablanca's diplomatic campaign designed to follow up the minis-

land, El Pardo, February 29, 1780, AHN, *Est.* 4220, *Expdte.* 2, Docs. 13, 14, 15, 16. For text see Appendix No. 3.

19 Fernan Nuñez to Floridablanca, Lisbon, February 24, 1780, *ibid.*, Doc. 11.

20 Floridablanca to Hussey, cipher, El Pardo, March 5, 1780, states that the Johnstone matter arrived at "the same time" as Hussey's of February 16, 1780. *ibid.*, Doc. 101. To indicate time of journey required by courier, note that Floridablanca knew on May 23 of Hussey and Cumberland's arrival at Lisbon, mentioned in Nuñez's dispatch of May 18 from that city, as well as in Hussey's own letter of that day. *ibid.*, Docs. 110, 32, 56.

terial decision of February 29 by a secret negotiation with England. For they professed to offer to Spain what the British Ministry orally had refused through Hussey. The new Johnstone "preliminary articles to serve as a basis for negotiation between England, Spain and France" proposed the arrangement of a tripartite peace at the very moment the British Government represented itself through Germain to Hussey as desiring a separate "individual" peace with Spain alone. The basis of the proposed three-power peace settlement was to be: (1) The American Colonies to have the status proposed by the British [Carlisle] peace commission of 1778—that is to say the status of 1763 which would have been acceptable to the Colonies before the Declaration of Independence and the French alliance, but which was now inacceptable to them except in defeat; (2) a mutual guaranty of possessions in America, to which the Court of Portugal would be invited to accede; (3) mutual restoration of conquests in Asia, Africa, and America; (4) cession of Gibraltar to Spain, who would pay for the munitions and artillery therein; (5) Spain to share equally with France in the fishing privileges in "Newfoundland Bay" by the treaty of Utrecht; (6) the treaty of Paris to be the basis of the present negotiation.[21]

These articles, proposed as the basis for a peace between Spain, England and France, were free from the imputation of a separate peace, and they presented a much better point of departure for Floridablanca than anything that had been sent by Hussey. But unfortunately their author had been expressly repudiated. Again, they did not provide for the principal object of

[21] Fernan Nuñez to Floridablanca, Lisbon, February 24, 1780, AHN, *Est.* 4220, *Expdte.* No. 2, Doc. 11, also Docs. 18, 19, 20, 21.

the Franco-American alliance, the independence of the
United States. But Floridablanca clung fondly to them.
He disliked to think that such pleasant and good articles
as these could really be disavowed. If they were, why was
not their author Johnstone visited with summary and
condign punishment by the august sovereign in whose
name he professed to speak? He saw, too, in these articles a means of satisfying France—under the interpretation of tacit independence—with some formula of
incomplete independence for the Colonies, to be fashioned out of the first Johnstone article. He therefore
proposed to England, by means of an autograph signed
letter addressed to Hussey, dated March 2, 1780, and
dispatched by way of Lisbon, that Spain offer her good
offices between England and France to bring about a
"mutually honorable settlement capable of fulfilling the
moderate views" of his Britannic Majesty; meanwhile
the British King "will undertake to complete a negotiation with the Colonies on such terms and stipulations as
to deprive them of just motives for claiming the succors
stipulated by the treaty of eventual alliance of February 6, 1778; and to achieve this will grant a suspension of arms, all the other belligerents promising not
to interfere with this negotiation unless such be proposed or requested by his Britannic Majesty."[22]

This proposition, if it had been accepted by France,
would have left England free to settle things alone with
the revolted Colonies deprived by such an armistice of
French aid.

As to the proposed territorial guaranty, it was to be
restricted to the territory of the respective belligerent
powers (not including Portugal), as fixed by the peace.

[22] For the Johnstone articles and Floridablanca's replies thereon, see
Appendix No. 4.

Johnstone's Gibraltar article was of course accepted, together with mutual restoration of conquests; but instead of a share in the French Newfoundland fisheries, Floridablanca proposed the cession of West Florida, leaving to England the part to the east of the entrance to the Bahama channel into the Gulf of Mexico, Spain getting back the western part located inside the Gulf of Mexico, giving something to England as an equivalent for this, if necessary. He also proposed to qualify the Treaty of Paris in principle by a stipulated restoration of Spanish authority over British woodcutters in Honduras. He added a seventh article to this effect: "If His Most Christian Majesty should accede to these preliminaries, the two Courts of London and Versailles will settle between themselves their respective interests according to their own convenience, and His [Catholic] Majesty on his side will make any *démarche* which might be agreeable to the two courts."[23]

In his autograph letter the Spanish Minister empowered Hussey to agree in principle with the British Ministry on a treaty between Spain and England covering these points. Another letter in cipher, embodying a digest of the same instructions went by way of the Spanish legation in Holland. Once accepted, the treaty was to be put in its final form at Lisbon, by the Spanish Ambassador there and such proper British plenipotentiary as might be designated for the purpose; or it could be done at The Hague, or even in London by a person to be designated by Spain for the purpose. "But from this instant," he charged Hussey, "you are

23 March 2, 1780, AHN, *Est.* 4220, *Expdte* 2, Doc. 20. See also Floridablanca to Hussey, El Pardo, March 2, 1780, *ibid.,* Doc. 94, a copy of which exists in Record Office, Foreign Office, Series 94, Vol. 209, pp. 1-9, containing Johnstone's six articles and Floridablanca's comments on them, as presented by Hussey in London.

authorized to treat and conclude this negotiation reserving only the exterior formalities for the persons and the places that I have suggested. As you are fully apprized of the recompense which we would give, I shall only add that should any doubts occur, they may be reserved for those who are to *extend*[24] the treaty at Lisbon." Hussey was to be careful to warn the British Ministry that Jay had already left Cadiz for Madrid, and that Floridablanca could not long hold off any negotiation with him.

The first Johnstone overtures of November 30, 1779, had been promptly communicated to the French Court. Nothing was said about these new ones. Hussey was expressly warned not to send any dispatches or even persons by way of France, in order to avoid exciting suspicions.[25] Even if eventual general peace settlement were professedly contemplated, Floridablanca was resolved to fix the terms of it for his French ally by preliminary secret negotiations with the enemy, just as France had presumed to do for Spain in the well remembered negotiations of 1763. France, presented with a *fait accompli,* would be forced to accept Spain's formula for a peace of her own with England.

The proposals sent to Hussey, by Lisbon and in duplicate cipher by Holland,[26] and the powers contained

24 Italics inserted.

25 Floridablanca to Hussey, cipher, El Pardo, March 5, 1780, AHN, *Est.* 4220, *Expdte.* 2, Doc. 101. This is the cipher dispatch which went by way of Holland.

26 Two dispatches were sent by way of Lisbon to Hussey, in Floridablanca's own handwriting and over his signatures, the one of February 29, and the other of March 2, 1780. Fernan Nuñez to Floridablanca, Lisbon, March 10, 1780, AHN, *Est.* 4220, *Expdte.* 2, Doc. 23. The dispatch of March 5, by way of Holland, was in cipher and did not have Floridablanca's signature. *ibid.,* Doc. 99 [letter of February 29, 1780], Doc. 94 [March 2], and Docs. 101, 102. A copy of the original autograph letter of March 2, 1780, was taken in England, where Hussey presumably showed it, and exists today in R.O., S.P.F., Series 194, Vol. 209. Letters

in them over Floridablanca's signature, were only to conclude the principal heads of a treaty; these were to be formalized *and extended* in Lisbon, The Hague or London, as the case might require. What he meant by the *extension* of the heads is to be seen in a set of thirteen proposed articles for Anglo-Spanish treaties, which Floridablanca drew up contemporaneously with the instructions to Hussey. These articles, together with the marginal comments on them, were to serve as instructions for the Spanish plenipotentiary who might be appointed. Seven articles were to be included in an open public treaty, *between Spain and England*: they simply provided for the conventional cessation of hostilities, mutual restoration of conquests, except West Florida; restriction of British settlements in Honduras and on the Campeche Coast; and a mixed commission to adjudicate Spanish spoliation claims arising before the declaration of war, a grievance which had been made much of in the Spanish manifesto accompanying the declaration. The final six articles were to be incorporated in a secret "exchange" treaty, upon the signature and ratification of which the signature and ratification of the public treaty were to depend. In these secret articles Gibraltar and Minorca were to be restored to Spain by way of compensation for the expenses of the war; the cession of Oran and Maralquivir [Mazalquivir] on the Barbary Coast was to be offered to England as an equivalent for Gibraltar, and, if necessary, a mixed commission would assess the value of stores at that fortress for payment by Spain to England. A marginal instruc-

of March 2 and 5, also signed by Floridablanca, on the subject of the exchange of prisoners masked the dispatches by Lisbon and by Holland. *ibid.*, Docs. 92, 100. For the text of the letters of February 29, March 2, and March 5 (via Holland), see Appendix No. 5.

tion urged the acquisition of Gibraltar if possible without such an equivalent; but should the British Ministry hold out for an equivalent, then Spain might throw in Oran and Maralquivir, providing Great Britain would add Port Mahon to Gibraltar.

It is the fourth, fifth, and sixth articles of the proposed secret exchange treaty—into which the British were to be led at Lisbon after committing themselves to the proposals placed in Hussey's hands in London— that arrest the attention of the student of American history. The points which were furnished to Hussey served as a basis for these, but Floridablanca introduced new phraseology which served to make Great Britain free to fix her own peace terms with the "Colonies" without the interference of Spain, or of France either. This was in the wording of Article VI of the proposed secret treaty:

"Whereas, His Britannic Majesty has been informed that the treaty of alliance and of recognition of the independence of the Colonies made by France the 6th of February, 1778, was eventual and conditional upon the contingency of England's *declaring* [italics inserted] war against France; and that consequently the force of that treaty (to which it is understood that the Most Christian King will never be unfaithful) depends on the same war, although this war has taken place in fact by way of reprisals, *without a formal declaration* [italics inserted]; this being the case His Britannic Majesty takes it upon himself in case His Most Christian Majesty accedes to the above treaty, to concert with the colonies in terms which can leave them no just grounds for claiming or complaining against France on the score of the stipulations of the said alliance, to which His Britannic Majesty will grant them a suspension of arms immediately, and for this purpose His Most Christian Majesty offers not to meddle directly or indirectly in the concert *or its consequences* [italics inserted]."

"France," added Floridablanca, in the margin, "obliges herself not to lay down arms until independence should be recognized, *expressly or tacitly.* The underscored words in this Article VI[27] appear to be such a tacit, even express recognition, once that the concert is put into terms that can give *no just claims on the alliance,* claims might be made without being recognized."

Here was the key which the genius of the Spanish Minister had forged! France need not be held up to the treaty of alliance with the United States because that alliance depended upon England having *declared* a war.[28] No war had been actually declared, though one existed. Hence France had no obligations of alliance to the United States, for the alliance was *eventual.* Through the casuistical use of the term *tacit* recognition, and the crafty distortion of the meaning of the word *just,* the great minister thought he had found the much needed formula by which France could be pushed through a painful loophole of escape from obligations to a depending and trustful ally and by which the primary objectives of Spain could be secured, along with lesser advantages. Under this theory the American Colonies would be really getting from France far more than they were strictly entitled to, if they should receive some arrangement of alleged tacit independence, which would

---

27 For complete text of this draft, and of the marginal comments, see Appendix No. 6.

28 The authoritative French text of the alliance reads: "*Au cas que la guerre se déclarât entre la France et la Grande Bretagne. . . .*" etc. The English text in the archives of the Department of State reads: "If war should break out between France and Great Britain. . . ." etc.

at the same time be a vague feudal dependence like that of the free cities of the Empire! A minister skilful in salving the conscience of his own king now sought to treat that of the King of France. This draft treaty and the marginal comments thereon remove all the shadows from the darker corners of Spanish diplomacy.

A final note for the guidance of the plenipotentiary stated that if a treaty were not concluded soon it would be too late. Mr. Jay was expected. Always the convenient Mr. Jay is made to appear in the offing, hastening to Madrid with a treaty of alliance which Floridablanca was about to sign. This seems the real reason why the Spanish Ministry was willing to furnish Jay a hundred and seventy thousand dollars to make possible his stay in Spain, even though he was not recognized by the Spanish Government. This time Floridablanca said nothing about the threatened imminent invasion of England—in vain the French were urging on him such a joint expedition. He pinned his hopes on the useful American, Mr. Jay, already on the road, Mr. Jay, hurrying on his way from Cadiz to Madrid.

In case France should not accept the proposed mediation of Spain, Floridablanca did not say what Spain would do; but the reader can draw only one conclusion.

This final draft for the proposed treaties, public and secret, with England, does not appear to have been sent to Hussey, though Fernan Nuñez was familiar with its contents.[29] Before there was occasion to appoint any plenipotentiary, news came that an accredited English agent had started for the Spanish Court, and in company with the redoubtable priest himself.

---

[29] Fernan Nuñez to Floridablanca, Lisbon, May 22, 1780, AHN, *Est.* 4220, *Expdte.* 2, Doc. 34.

CHAPTER IV

THE HUSSEY-CUMBERLAND VENTURE

"YOUR letter by way of Holland arrived and the same day I informed the Secretary of State of the corresponding department, who communicated it straightway to the King of England; and His Britannic Majesty, seeing that his royal name is still being employed in regard to you, from Lisbon, without authority, and desiring to proceed with this peace negotiation quickly and secretly, for which he seems much pressed, gives plenipotentiary powers to Secretary [sic] Cumberland, whom he has nominated to Your Excellency as a subject very friendly to an agreement, the same person who saw me first on the part of Lord George Germain. He will go to Lisbon immediately in a warship; and since the King of Great Britain thinks that it might facilitate the negotiation for me to accompany him, I have consented to it, hoping that I shall not merit the disapprobation of Yourself."[1]

Such was Hussey's description of the answer of the British Government to the propositions which Floridablanca had made on the basis of Johnstone's discredited proposals. It had set aside the ideas of Johnstone, but had not refused to send a man to Spain to talk peace after Floridablanca had announced a program which was really based on those proposals.

Richard Cumberland, who up to this time had served merely as a go-between for Hussey's conversations with

[1] Hussey to Floridablanca, London, March 28, 1780, AHN, *Est.* 4220, *Expdte.* 2, Doc. 105.

Germain, was a second-rate dramatist of the English sentimental school, a man who looked down on Sheridan. A playwright whose voluminous dramatic works, most of them never long played even in their own time, have long since been forgotten, he was a writer of "achievement without the divine fire; of industry without inspiration; of strong and varied talents without genius."[2] He came from a family of distinguished clerics, one of whom, his paternal great-grandfather, was that Bishop Cumberland, scholar and philosopher, who is remembered as a friend of Pepys; another, his maternal grandfather, was none less than the famous classical scholar, Bentley, master of Trinity College. Himself actually born in the master's lodge of Trinity College, right under Bentley's study, Richard Cumberland's whole early life was a willing grind over books, most of them classical literature, which turned him out a good enough classicist, but shut out from his mind the more spontaneous and lively qualities which come from contacts with other less learned but more bracing currents of life. So labored and so perfected were his classical studies as to give him words without feeling for them, form without lilt or music in it. Nor did sedulous imitation of Latin literary styles elevate him within reach of any sublimity of expression. In short, bookish young Cumberland grew up in the study and remained more or less a pedant all his life. After he left Cambridge he became a professional placeman, dependent on the patronage of various noble lords. First it was as secretary to Lord Halifax—then as Ulster Secretary when Halifax in 1761 became Lord Lieutenant for Ireland; but when his master became a cabinet member in

---

[2] Stanley T. Williams, *Richard Cumberland, His Life and Dramatic Works* (New Haven, 1917), 1.

1762 he dropped Cumberland, who had expected the under-secretaryship, telling him coldly that "he was not fit for every situation."[3] So Cumberland, now possessed of a wife and growing family, had to content himself with a lower clerkship left by the man who succeeded him in Halifax's favor, that of clerk of the records in the Board of Trade. He managed, however, to keep the agency for the Colony of Nova Scotia, an appointment bringing £200 a year which had fallen to him.[4] The light labors of the new job gave Cumberland time to write and an opportunity to cultivate the favor of Lord Hillsborough, president of the Board of Trade, and to become obsequious to other members of the Board, like Lord George Germain. Thanks to Germain's favor Cumberland eventually succeeded Thomas Pownall in 1775, as secretary of the Board. A livelihood dependent on the favors of ruling aristocrats made of Cumberland a typical placeman, but distinctive because of his literary industry. It gave him no real insight into the controlling forces of human character, no key to the mastery of men. Despite his increasing literary reputation, he never ceased to marvel at the parts and manners of men and women moving above his plane. He respected those on whom he was dependent. He modelled his carriage and deportment after them. Toward souls beneath his secretarial and literary stratum he looked with a mingling of cold reserve and satirical amusement. He was no Beaumarchais. The eighteenth century English social system kept him uncomplainingly in his place and prompted him with the conventional superciliousness and assumption of lordly quali-

[3] *Memoirs of Richard Cumberland Written by Himself* (London, 1807); I, 242.

[4] He had also been Provost Marshal of South Carolina until 1768, an office which he tried in vain to commute into ready cash. Williams, *op. cit.*, 59.

ties when no lord was present to see and control. A man whose political experience had been limited to the art of pleasing patrons and impressing little people, a man without political imagination or real knowledge of the world, a pedantic and impressionable literary person, this was the Cumberland whom the British Ministry chose to send to Spain under the wing of the subtle Hussey, to deal with the experienced Floridablanca.

Though one is inclined to account for the curious appointment of Cumberland for such a difficult task in the same way that one accounts for Germain's appointment of General Burgoyne—sheer ineptitude of a cabinet minister,—it is not impossible that he may have been chosen because of his proven subordinate nature. In this case his principals failed to foresee the effects of the zeal which their newly sponsored diplomatist would let loose on foreign soil.

All that Cumberland's instructions allowed him to do was to propose a peace on the basis of the Treaty of Paris, with an added stipulation that Spain must bind herself against all aid, or commerce or intercourse in any way with the revolted Americans, and close her ports and realms to them absolutely. He was allowed to listen *ad referendum* to any propositions that the Spanish Ministry might make for the cession of territory other than Gibraltar or Minorca; but he was specifically forbidden to discuss Spanish propositions for mediation either between Great Britain and the revolted Colonies on the one hand, or between Great Britain and France on the other. The most therefore that England now offered was the *status quo ante bellum* coupled with a humiliating renunciation by Spain of any aid to or commerce with the Americans; in return for this, some minor territorial rearrangements might be allowed, such as an exchange of Florida for Porto Rico and perhaps withdrawal of British claims on the Honduran coast. The most important injunctions of the instructions forbade Cumberland even to depart from Lisbon for the Spanish Court unless Hussey, who was to visit the Court in advance of Cumberland, should send back specific word that the Spanish Minister had no intention nor expectation of securing by cession or exchange either Gibraltar or Minorca. Then, and only then, might Cumberland set out for Spain; and if such specific assurances should not arrive within twenty-one days he was to return to London.[5] The ship's captain had orders not to wait in Lisbon any longer. Since an average carriage journey from Lisbon to Madrid required about ten days—though couriers made it in five —the margin of time was sufficiently parsimonious to be impressive.

Though Hussey posed to the British Ministry as a sincere and holy man whose sole purpose was to satisfy his friendship to both countries by bringing about peace between the two, his real character was of course known to the Ministry when they sent him to Spain along with the inexperienced Cumberland. The restricted character of Cumberland's instructions, together with the fact that he bore no cipher and intrusted nearly all his mail to the open post or to Spanish couriers, makes it plain that

[5] For Cumberland's instructions, dated April 17, 1780, see R.O., S.P.F., Series 94, Vol. 209. A copy of the autograph letter of instruction is in *ibid.*; the original is in AHN, *Est.* 4220, *Expdte.* 2, Doc. 155. A draft treaty of seven articles is filed with Cumberland's instructions. It provides for a separate peace on the basis of the Treaty of Paris of 1763, and for the exchange of West Florida for the island of Porto Rico. The time limit for the frigate is inferred from Cumberland's private letters to Hillsborough, from Portsmouth, April 21, and from Lisbon, May 29, R.O., S.P.F., class 94, Vol. 209, pp. 47, 65; and Fernan Nuñez to Floridablanca, Lisbon, May 22, 1780, AHN, *Est.* 4220, *Expdte.* 2, Doc. 34.

Hussey was used to emphasize to the Spanish Ministry by virtue of his complete knowledge of Cumberland's purposes, that Great Britain would treat only on the basis of the Treaty of Paris, with certain minor territorial cessions, and a Spanish disavowal of any connection with the American rebels. There was doubtless no objection to Hussey's copying off Cumberland's instructions, and worming out of him anything he could. He would only find the agent tied down to terms advantageous to England. No harm could be done; something might be gained if the Spaniards should listen to peace on such a basis.

In this respect Hussey certainly did his duty. He had already been improving his time in London, while waiting for Floridablanca's propositions, by corrupting minor officials and sending in secret reports to his chief; and he continued to make his reports after he had been allotted the acceptable task of being companion to Cumberland.[6] On the voyage he managed to get copies of all of Cumberland's instructions, which he hurried on to Floridablanca the minute he got on shore at Lisbon. Before he mailed Cumberland's dispatches to Madrid he sent ahead letters saying by what couriers or routes they might be expected, in order to assist their prompt interception. All the more important correspondence between Cumberland and Hillsborough during the mission was copied off by Hussey and put in the hands of Bernardo del Campo, Floridablanca's English-speaking secretary, or else it was easily available in the mails. But then, this was a part of the game, and was, we repeat, doubtless expected by the British Government, if

6 Hussey to Floridablanca, London, March 8 (cipher), March 28 (two dispatches, one in cipher), April 10 (cipher), April 13 (cipher), 1780, AHN, *Est.* 4220, *Expdte.* 2, Docs. 103, 104, 105, 107, 109.

not by Cumberland himself, who remained together with his family, on the most friendly and even affectionate terms with the priest, whose amiable social qualifications and natural gallantry were not the least of his many abilities.

After some waiting for fair winds, during which time Cumberland purposely walked Hussey through the naval arsenals at Portsmouth[7] to give him, on the eve of his journey to Madrid, a proper impression of British naval strength, the *Milford* frigate, Captain William Burnaby, stood out to sea at eight o'clock on the morning of April 28, 1780.[8] With Cumberland went his wife and two grown daughters. Another infant daughter was to be born in Spain before the hot summer had passed. Four sons were serving under His Majesty's colors on land and sea in various parts of the world. For the impressionable Cumberlands—and indeed it would have been for anybody else except a hardened traveller like Hussey—it was an exciting voyage. As land began to drop from sight the ship sprung its mizzen-mast below the trussel-trees. No sooner was this repaired than a big storm came up, on the 9th, which disabled and nearly foundered the frigate. They remembered it long afterward by reason of having seen the massive frame of Hussey catapulted through the ship's wardroom to demolish everything with which he came in contact, including a fiddler who was trying to lull the nerves of the uneasy passengers. The crew had hardly left the pumps when a French privateer was sighted. A sharp engagement followed and the Frenchman had to strike his ensign. Three of the *Milford's* crew were killed. A

[7] Cumberland to Germain, Portsmouth, April 21, 1780, *Stopford-Sackville Papers*, I, 332.

[8] It did not get past Land's End until the sixth of May.

sailor gallantly and unflinchingly presented the sleeved stump of a freshly mangled arm to Cumberland's eldest daughter as, descending the ship's unsteady gangway, he met her during the action. Cumberland read the rites of the Church of England at the burial service of a Protestant sailor the next day; and Hussey officiated for two Irishmen. The scuppers washed down and the ship under way again with the prize in tow, Cumberland composed an appropriate ballad. He claims in his *Memoirs,* written twenty-five years later, that the "very musically inclined" crew sang it right lustily on the remainder of the voyage and in Lisbon. In his new capacity of a diplomatic envoy with a frigate at his service, Cumberland took it upon himself to pen to the Earl of Hillsborough an unavailing letter recommending for promotion the frigate's first officer, for gallantry in action.

Finally the *Milford* dropped anchor off Belem Castle in the Tagus on the evening of the 17th of May. The next morning Hussey landed, had some conferences with Fernan Nuñez, and learned that the latter was pretty well apprised of the business of Cumberland's mission. He had received word from Floridablanca to whom Hussey had sent dispatches from England before the *Milford's* departure.[9] By Nuñez's courier the Abbé informed Floridablanca of his and Cumberland's arrival. Early on the morning of the 19th of May the priest himself set out for Aranjuez, where the Spanish Court was tarrying during the last beautiful weeks of spring. Meanwhile Johnstone came in to Lisbon and took general command over the *Milford* as one of the British ships anchored on his station. He talked with Cantofer

---

[9] Hussey to Floridablanca, London, March 28, 1780, AHN, *Est.* 4220, *Expdte.* 2, Doc. 105.

some more, and Cantofer with Fernan Nuñez, who sent on to Floridablanca Johnstone's distorted version of the arrival of the frigate and of the personages on board. These emissaries according to Johnstone were bringing assurance that England was actually ready to deliver over Gibraltar, and to cede West Florida. Johnstone had further asserted that Cumberland had instructions to confer with him, Johnstone (former Governor of West Florida), about the cession of that province. The expressive Commodore was frank to say that he would advise against such a cession, "because of the importance of the post, but the more so because he had his principal estates and indigo plantations in the neighborhood of Baton Rouge, now in the possession of Spain, and for which he had the greatest hopes and expectations, so that he would never consent to anything which might damage them so much." Nuñez hastened to assure Johnstone, always through Cantofer, that the King would doubtless provide adequate "compensation" for any such losses, "particularly if on his [Johnstone's] part he should have contributed in some way to the achievement of his upright intentions." Nuñez never construed this as a commitment, nor did Floridablanca, and the British naval officer's greatest hopes and expectations remained unsatisfied. Putting together the Johnstone conversations with what Hussey had said to him, Fernan Nuñez advised Floridablanca that he thought the English envoy would hold out against the cession of Gibraltar, but that he might eventually be brought to it through some guise of exchange, such as Gibraltar for Oran, or maybe for West Florida— Nuñez was against giving England any foothold on the Barbary Coast. He did not think it possible to get Port Mahon, too, according to Floridablanca's previous ideas.[10] Johnstone's suggestive conversations with Canto-fer seemed the more plausible because of the self-interest which they manifested. Thus it appeared to the Spanish Minister that when the cards should all be put on the table the British would actually yield the great fortress. Such news came up from the Lisbon embassy by the time that Hussey reached Aranjuez, May 28.

The Abbé immediately got in contact with Campo, delivered over copies of Cumberland's papers and put at the disposal of his superiors the information which he had brought back from England. Compared with Nuñez's reports, it was all disappointing. "It appears to me that the negotiation has gone infinitely backward from the first word, as you will see from the secret copy of the instructions which Cumberland carries," reported Campo to his chief.[11]

Should Cumberland be invited to come on to the Spanish Court, by sending him the required assurances which Hussey had been instructed to get? Keeping in the back of his mind the idea that, once the English emissary were got hold of in Madrid, circumstances might develop so as to bring forth a peace in which (as Floridablanca had originally conceived) Gibraltar could be ceded by a secret treaty of exchange, the Minister composed a message for Hussey to send, accompanied by passports for the whole family, to the waiting Cumberland. This message by no means gave the required assurance. "On my arrival here I visited

10 Fernan Nuñez to Floridablanca, Lisbon, May 22, 1780, AHN, *Est.* 4220, *Expdte.* 2, Doc. 34. This document shows that Nuñez knew of the draft instructions which Floridablanca had drawn up for the plenipotentiary intended ultimately to treat with the British agent, and that he had probably been instructed to treat with a British plenipotentiary on that basis, should one appear *in Lisbon.*

11 Memorandum by Campo to Floridablanca, Sunday night, May 28, AHN, *Est.* 4220, *Expdte.* 2, Doc. 160.

the Minister,"—thus began the text of a little "outline" which Floridablanca penned for Hussey to send (in
slightly varying texts) to Cumberland and to Hillsborough. "He spoke of the delay and of the different
aspect and appearance which affairs continue to take
each day, making the negotiation more arduous and
difficult. Nevertheless, this Minister being very desirous
of finding some way to follow up and finish happily
this negotiation, and willing to have Cumberland come
for this purpose, under the pretext of passing through
Spain on the way to Italy for the health of his family,
it seemed imprudent in me not to agree to this; and
I accordingly wrote in those terms to Cumberland. As
for me I shall cultivate as much as possible these desires."[12] Meanwhile Floridablanca wrote to Fernan
Nuñez to keep open the secret conversations with Johnstone,—circumstances might shift so that at an oppor-
tune moment the principal matter (Gibraltar) could be
brought forward at the right time. "Whether he [Cum-
berland] brings the powers and instructions which Johnstone says, we shall see; but if he does not bring them,
or comes not hither, nothing is lost."

These conversations between Cantofer and Johnstone
continued during Cumberland's sojourn at Lisbon and
after his departure for Spain, and they further convinced Fernan Nuñez that as a last recourse England
would yield Gibraltar in the impending negotiations.[13]
This undoubtedly encouraged Floridablanca.

[12] AHN, *Est.* 4220, *Expdte.* 2, Docs. 152, 153.

[13] On May 30 Floridablanca wrote Fernan Nuñez approving of his conversations and his operations through Cantofer, and conveying the expression of the Minister's personal esteem for the latter. "Although the English
affect secrecy and a desire to negotiate, everything indicates the contrary, and they can make up the time they have lost only when the aspect
of things varies so that we can do there what we would have done in other
circumstances. I indicated to them the end of February as a limit when

It was now Hussey's task to get Cumberland to Madrid despite the instructions which demanded absolute assurances that Gibraltar would not enter into the negotiations. He wrote him as Floridablanca directed, varying slightly the wording: "However as the Minister is exceedingly desirous of finding some means to bring it to a happy conclusion: and as you are already so far advanced upon your journey, I think it by all means advisable that you come (giving out that you mean to pass thro' Spain to Italy for the benefit of your health),

they approached me at the end of December, and up to the middle of May they have not put in appearance." After summarizing the military events which had occurred meanwhile, Floridablanca says: "It is all right for Your Excellency and Cantofer to go ahead on this basis, acting opportunely and wisely, and keeping the main thing secret because even if they do not do so, we should do so ourselves, since we have offered to [*Conviene que V.E. y Cantofer caminen sobre estos principios para hacer uso con sagicidad oportuna, sin faltar al secreto de lo principal; pues aunque no lo guarden ellos, debemos guardarlo nosotros ya que lo hemos ofrecido*]. The order is going forth for Your Excellency to permit Cumberland to come to Spain and to give him passports. Incidentally we may settle the point of exchange [of prisoners] in order not to have to treat with that blusterer of an English Consul. Your Excellency will use this pretext, as already understood, with the French *chargé* or with any others who may possibly discuss Cumberland's possible detention here. Whether he brings the powers and instructions which Johnstone says, we shall see; but if he does not bring them, or comes not hither, nothing is lost." AHN, *Est.* 4220, *Expdte.* 2, Doc. 35. In his letter of June 22, 1780, to Floridablanca, recounting more conversations between Cantofer and Johnstone, Fernan Nuñez reports: "From Johnstone's propositions, and those of Cumberland, he [Cantofer] infers just what I have intimated in my correspondence with Your Excellency: that they are not averse to giving up Gibraltar, but pretending to yield it as a last recourse. The former told him that only in case of a failure of Clinton's expedition against Carolina, or some great disaster to Rodney's squadron, would Cumberland according to his instructions be able to treat of Gibraltar; and the latter commissioner assured him that Johnstone had been proceeding irresponsibly and against his instructions in proposing the cession of the place for one of the preliminary articles of negotiations, since although they were not absolutely opposed to admitting it, it was essential to get first a majority in Parliament and convince them that this is the only way to form a union in good faith with Spain with benefit to her own commerce and overseas possessions." *ibid.,* Doc. 38.

and so to give the negotiation a fair tryal. You know
me too well to suspect that I shall be wanting to cultivate the good wishes of the Minister of State, and to
incline him towards an accommodation. My servant
Daly carrys a *memorandum* of the road, and the different places where the relays of carriages are to meet
you."[14] The memorandum of travelling directions described the way as far as Aranjuez, *"where everything
else* [the words were twice underscored by the Abbé],
as well as my heart, will be ready to receive you and
your family. . . . It is unnecessary to tell you with what
impatience I await your arrival, to see once more my
dearest Friends, and to tell you a 1,000 things *which I
do not write.*"[15] By Daly, Hussey's servant who took
the letters from Aranjuez to Lisbon, the Abbé sent a
cryptic oral message: "All is well."[16]

There was no guaranty, in any of these words which
Hussey conveyed to Cumberland, that the subject of
Gibraltar and Minorca would not enter into the discussions. Floridablanca certainly meant to bring up that
subject and to make Gibraltar the basis of any peace.
This much is clearly evidenced in another of his secret
memoranda of ideas for Hussey to give out: "All we
[i.e., we, the English!] can hope for is that this might
not be mentioned in the treaty of peace nor in the preliminaries, but the Spanish Cabinet will insist always
that this be adjusted by means of an exchange, or some

14 Hussey to Cumberland, Aranjuez, May 31, 1780, R.O., S.P.F., Series
94, Vol. 209, p. 110. Printed in Cumberland's *Memoirs,* II, 9. A Spanish
copy was delivered to Campo. AHN, *Est.* 4220, *Expdte.* 2, Doc. 114.

15 Memorandum for Mr. Cumberland's Journey, R.O., S.P.F., Series 94,
Vol. 209, p. 111. See Appendix No. 7. A Spanish copy was delivered to
Campo. AHN, *Est.* 4220, *Expdte.* 2, Doc. 114.

16 Cumberland to Hussey, Lisbon, June 6, 1780, R.O., S.P.F., Series 94,
Vol. 209, p. 69.

other recompense, and desires that one and the other treaty be signed at the same time." But this memorandum, which we shall examine presently, was not shown to Cumberland until after he reached the Spanish Court, and a copy does not appear ever to have been forwarded to the British Government, either by Hussey or by Cumberland.

Meanwhile Cumberland, anxious to go on with his mission, was impatiently waiting at Lisbon with his family, enduring the trials of extreme hot weather and lack of sanitation, sampling the sights and novelties of the capital, and writing long descriptive letters home to Lord George Germain, as if that war minister did not have enough to peruse in the dispatches from his American generals.[17]

The "clear and candid judgement" of Lord George Germain for the help of which Cumberland yearned, in Lisbon, had not been noted for its infallibility ever since the affair of Minden in 1759, and it was particularly insecure when working at long distances, as had been exemplified in the preparations for the Saratoga campaign in 1777. There was no chance for Cumberland to avail himself even of this slender reed, for on June 6 Hussey's message arrived. The dramatist was eager to advance, too zealous for a great diplomatic achievement.

[17] "My Heart moreover is so fixt upon my business, and my hope of Success is so warm, that I feel no difficulties and fear no dangers. I am closely watch'd, but I know it, and know the Spies that are set upon me; Thus forewarn'd, I am forearm'd, and tho' I have no Soul to advise with, apprehend nothing either for myself or my business. Of a certain I shoud be delighted, if I coud slip into your Cabinet for one Hour, and avail myself in this exigency of that clear and candid Judgement which at once possesses me of both Head and Heart, & gives both comfort & counsel at the Same time—But my Lot has fallen upon other ground, and I must be silent. I beseech of God to bless you and your sweet family, whom I love with the tenderest respect and affection. . . ." Cumberland to Lord George Germain, May 26, 1780, *Stopford-Sackville Papers*, I, 334.

Because Hussey had not said that Spain stipulated for Gibraltar, he did not consider himself under orders to return to England. But the holy man had not said that Spain would treat without that fortress. Cumberland therefore was exceedingly doubtful whether he was warranted to advance from Lisbon. He consulted with Robert Walpole, British Minister in Portugal, who had been made cognizant of the business. This professional diplomatist advised against going to Madrid; there had been no express renunciation of Gibraltar. Searching for excuses, Cumberland found comfort in the vague but pleasing hints that Hussey had thrown out: the fact that Daly had brought the oral message "all is well," that Hussey had kept back things to say which he did not write, that "everything else," as well as the priest's heart, awaited him at Aranjuez, that he ought to give the negotiation a "fair tryal." He convinced himself that he might insult the Spanish Court if he refused to accept the passports which had been sent ahead to him and his whole family. In short he decided to go, even though it were against the letter of his instructions. The decision was a mistake, even though it was approved later by Hillsborough. By undertaking forthwith the journey to Madrid the ingenuous Cumberland was playing directly into the hands of Floridablanca and the good Hussey. The family and retainers, a little cavalcade, started en route, June 8, for the Spanish frontier.

CHAPTER V

CUMBERLAND AT THE COURT OF SPAIN

"How could you suspect that I would send for you if I found the obstacle in my way, which makes you so uneasy?" asked Hussey in a letter from the Court which greeted Cumberland as he arrived at Talavera la Reina on June 16. The good priest longed to embrace his amiable friend and to open his mind fully to his own satisfaction and pleasure. Let Cumberland hasten on. "I did not hesitate to risque this journey, even against the advice of Mr. W[alpole]," exultantly replied Cumberland as he and his weary family prepared for the last lap of the dusty journey.[1] On Sunday the 18th of June, 1780, at 5 o'clock in the morning the travellers reached the *real sitio* of Aranjuez, where the gardens were heavy with the fullness of summer odors, and the greenish Tagus lined with royal boathouses gained headway towards the distant sea.

In the fertile meadows of Aranjuez, or among the plashing fountains and geometrical gardens on the mountainside of La Granja, or on the dry and windy autumnal plains of the Pardo, the Spanish royal family lived in serenity and insouciance while empires trembled and new states were born. No pleasure, no calamity, could interrupt the imperturbable peregrinations of the Court seasonally from one royal estate to the next. No

---

[1] Hussey to Cumberland, Aranjuez, Wednesday morning, June 14, 1780; Cumberland to Hussey, Talavera la Reina, Friday, June 16, half-past 5 evening, *Memoirs,* II, 30. 31. The *Memoirs* give an entertaining account of the family's travel under primitive conditions of transport from Lisbon to Aranjuez.

serious business could interfere with the royal hunting parties. Perhaps only in the harsh gloom of the shadows of the stony Escorial, brooding over the remains of Bourbon forbears, or maybe in the hot, steamy and populous city of Madrid, could a Spanish monarch really fix his thoughts seriously on problems of war and diplomacy. But if monarchs dallied, ministers were always busy in Spain, even at the side of the indolent Court. The ascetic Floridablanca was ever at labor, his mind full of lucubrations that might fix the future of millions of men on two continents across a span of seas. Even now a representative of three millions, struggling against the attempts of England to keep them dependent on the British crown, was hopefully trailing the Spanish Court about Castile. The diplomatic corps was now with the Court at Aranjuez, and among them was watchful young Montmorin, the French Ambassador. Already they were awake to rumors[2] of the advent of Cumberland, and diplomatists walking under the great trees along the river in the cool of the evening were speculating on the significance of his mission. Suddenly the London playwright stepped out on the stage of the diplomatic world of a European court, whose characters were far more real and more portentous than the voluble beings and pompous puppets of his sentimental dramas.

Would Spain make a separate peace with the enemy? Already Montmorin had begun to suspect that some fire was to be found beneath the fumes of Johnstone's loud talk at Lisbon. Not doubting for a moment his ambassador's suspicions, Vergennes gave orders for the retirement of the incompetent French *chargé* at Lisbon who

[2] Francesco Pesaro (Venetian Ambassador) to the Senate, No. 203, Aranjuez, June 21, 1780, *Archivio di Stato* (Venice), *Dispacci, Spagna, Filza* 180.

had been too easily deceived by Fernan Nuñez.[3] "Anything is possible," wrote Vergennes to Montmorin, "Now is the time to redouble your vigilance."[4]

So far the French had not suspected the real and most important channel—Cumberland and Hussey. When Floridablanca knew by the latter's messages from London that an English agent was to be sent to Lisbon or Madrid, it was obvious that as soon as such a person might be appointed it would be no longer possible to conceal the negotiation. He therefore straightway (April 14, 1780) informed Vergennes confidentially,[5] keeping the information from Aranda, who did not receive any official notice of it until four months later. A further show of confidence was made at this same time—the middle of April, while Cumberland and Hussey were preparing to embark from England—in communicating to the French Ambassador at Madrid and to the American agent, John Jay, a copy of a windy memorandum which an Englishman, Sir John Dalrymple, then travelling through Spain, had delivered to Floridablanca. The reasons for Dalrymple's Spanish passports

[3] Vergennes to Montmorin, private, March 31, 1780, Doniol, IV, 450. Speaking of the arrival of Cumberland and Hussey at Lisbon and the latter's departure for Madrid, Fernan Nuñez notes to Floridablanca, May 22, 1780: "The French *chargé d'affaires* told me he knew of his [Hussey's] trip to Madrid through the same merchant Pasley, to whom he had been recommended from England and who furnished him with necessary money. I thought that making a mystery of it would give him [the *chargé*] just reason for suspicions; and confessing it to him right away, I told him with the greatest reserve, that it was a matter of treating for the exchange of prisoners in which there were some difficulties to conquer; and that since a good many of these came from the English consul here, it would not be well to have the matter known here or elsewhere while it was not entirely settled, with which he remained satisfied, pleased and tranquil." AHN, *Est.* 4220, *Expdte.* 2, Doc. 34. Cumberland and Hussey did have a little to do with some exchanges of prisoners.

[4] Doniol, IV, 450.

[5] *ibid.*, 451.

at this moment are not to be explained, nor the peace suggestions embodied in this verbose memorandum. But the fact that he is only incidentally mentioned in the official correspondence of Cumberland, and not at all by Hussey; that his passage through Spain was a very flying one; that his memorandum was promptly communicated by Floridablanca to Montmorin and to Jay; that its character—though curiously resembling some features of Johnstone's second set of articles—was too academic to have any direct relation to the problems then being considered by the British Cabinet and the Spanish Ministry,—all these features suggest that Dalrymple, habitually given to much officious letter writing and publication, was acting on his own responsibility. Like Johnstone, Dalrymple, who had arrived at the Spanish Court on April 9, represented himself as an intimate of Lord North. His proposed peace settlement, outlined in a lengthy document entitled *"Anecdote Historique,"* was based on a four-power (Great Britain, France, Portugal, and Spain) guaranty of colonial territorial integrity; common participation in colonial commerce "under the limitation of its being not incompatible with the common interests of English America and England," and a "Magna Carta to the liberties of America." According to Jay, the Spanish Minister spoke of the memoir "properly . . . and concluded with assurances of the King's firmness."[6] Montmorin felt that Dalrymple was without powers except to exhibit the facility with which peace might be made.[7] Floridablanca's lavish confidences concerning the contents of the Dalrymple memoir contrast strikingly with the inviolable secrecy of the peace terms which had passed be-

---

[6] Wharton, III, 727-731, gives copy of the document.
[7] Doniol, IV, 455.

tween himself and the British Cabinet by way of Hussey. Whatever his mission in Spain, Dalrymple afforded Floridablanca a chance to make an innocuous gesture of loyalty. It impressed the Americans but was without effect on the French. From this time on Vergennes was in a constant state of alarm at the possibility of a separate Spanish peace, as well he might have been. He began immediately to canvass ways and means to meet such a step and to find a gateway of diplomatic retreat should that be necessary. Casting about in desperation he espied a narrow exit, the one in fact through which Floridablanca intended to drive him—*tacit* independence for the American Colonies. But it will be more convenient to consider in a separate chapter the implications for American independence of Floridablanca's peace formula. For the present let us observe the diplomatic endeavors of Richard Cumberland and his *compagnon de voyage* the Irish priest, that Spanish vassal, Thomas Hussey.

After his usual manner Floridablanca prepared for the conversations with Cumberland. He wrote another memorandum for Hussey's use, again curiously couched as though it were in the mouth of a British agent. The repeated use of such phraseology implies that the Spanish Minister actually believed that Hussey was regarded in England as a genuine British agent! This memorandum is not to be found in the English archives. Cumberland states that immediately after his arrival at Aranjuez Hussey under the strictest confidence showed him the "paper" in Floridablanca's own hand. Since Cumberland did not read Spanish, and since he did not retain a copy, we may conclude that he relied on Hussey for an oral English rendition. In that case Hussey must have omitted the first person pronouns in which Floridablanca originally wrote it to make it appear as Hussey's paper. A copy of this interesting document in its original form, as exhibited to Cumberland, and now in the *Archivo Histórico Nacional* at Madrid, is included in the appendix to this volume.[8] This was the cue given by the Spanish Foreign Minister to Cumberland as he stepped on the stage at Aranjuez.

Hussey (that is, Floridablanca) reported in this memorandum what seemed to him "the line of thought by which the war may be cut short and the Court of London brought out of its present circumstances." The delay of the negotiation beyond the end of February, the time limit stipulated during Hussey's first trip, had resulted in changed conditions, with victories and defeats for both powers at sea and overseas, and in the arrival and incessant importunities of Jay for a Spanish alliance. These delays had made the Spanish Court distrustful, though originally it had been most favorable to a peace negotiation "according to the terms which I communicated to Lord George Germain . . . possibly because it presumes that, what with the rumors, and the overtures which have been scattered about in Lisbon and elsewhere, we are trying to lull them to sleep in order to strike them blows in Spain and in Spanish possessions, and to create bad feelings between them and France." The various military and naval events which had happened, and which were balanced philosophically against each other in the memorandum, together with the vigorous promises which the Americans were making, "have increased the difficulties which exist here in undertaking a favorable negotiation because of the good intentions of this sovereign, who according to all my information certainly desires, if I am not much mistaken,

[8] See Appendix No. 8.

to find some honorable and decent way of giving peace to Europe. The compassionate and religious character of this prince itself leads to that desire, but his natural firmness and jealousy in points of honor, which some measure as extraordinary obstinacy, impede flexibility on many points especially if His Majesty thinks they may be against the honor or engagement of his word and obligations." There existed three principal points for the Spanish Ministry to consider: (1) whether or not to include France in the negotiation, (2) how to include or exclude the Colonies, (3) whether Gibraltar is to be ceded. As to the first point, it seems impossible that Spain will lend herself to any separate peace and abandonment of France. It was much more difficult, anyway, to treat separately now that Cumberland's arrival had been announced in Lisbon and even in Paris. The Spanish Ministry suspected that this was artificial publicity created to separate France and Spain, but nevertheless if Great Britain should find some way to satisfy Spain and to concert a decent settlement with France, it might be hoped that if France should not accede to it, the Spanish Ministry would conceivably do so. Then further negotiations might lessen the force of the Franco-Spanish union. This, "Hussey" believed, was a most important point for England; if a peace settlement could include the three powers in a mutual guaranty of territory in all parts of the world, Spain could not after that draw her sword against England.

As to the second point, the American Colonies, Spain had not yet contracted with them, and therefore could make a settlement with England without including the Colonies; but France would never let this point drop out of sight, at least would want to save appearances. And Spain could not decently propose to France "openly" to go back on her engagements made, for better or worse, with the Colonies. For this reason some "middle term" must be found, and it was suggested that for this "England affirm and offer that she will herself alone compound and adjust with the Congress or with the Colonies *in terms which will not enable the latter to make claim on France for the observance of her treaties.*" With these expressions everything could be saved; for if England should settle by a recovery of dependence, the Colonies, having consented to it, could not accuse France; and if in their adjustment they should get independence so much the less would they be able to complain against France. The argument continued:

"As to the third point, the cession of Gibraltar, it seems to me that all we can hope for is that this might not be mentioned in the treaty of peace nor in the preliminaries, but the Spanish Court will insist always that this be adjusted by a separate treaty by means of an exchange, or some other recompense, and desire that one and the other treaty be signed at the same time. In the separate treaty could be included a general guaranty by both Crowns of their dominions in Europe and in America, and even reciprocal assistance in case of invasion. Also it would be possible to obtain advantages of commerce, which I intimated formerly, at least to the extent of favors enjoyed by France.

"Unless Gibraltar is agreed to Spain can never become a true friend of England, for the Spanish nation will always long for its recovery, and the Ministry will be drawn into war on every occasion favorable for a rupture; but on the other hand if that object of discord is removed everything will conspire to give hope for much union between the two nations, who will see themselves without rivalry, which will not be the case with the French themselves.

"I will not undertake to give advice upon the line which Mr. Cumberland and his Court will take on these points; but my opinion would be to consult upon all these matters which it may be desirable for the English Ministry to discuss, in order that he may say what it is desired to do in case the negotiation should continue, or in case it should break off."

Therefore he was advising Cumberland to come to Spain, with the passports offered him, under pretext of passing to Italy, or perhaps sojourning in a Spanish province, like Valencia, for the health of his family.

This reads like the substance of a letter to the British Ministry, but, we repeat, there is no evidence that it was shown to anybody else but Cumberland, and presumably Cumberland got its sense only in Hussey's oral translation.[9] Certainly an unmistaken translation of the full text of this document should have made it perfectly plain to Cumberland that his negotiation could not proceed along the terms of his instructions, that is, omitting any reference to Gibraltar, the American Colonies, or France. It should have convinced him that he had been deceived in coming to the Spanish Court on Hus-

[9] Hillsborough reproved Cumberland for having delivered a written reply to this paper, and for not having sent a copy of it home to London. Cumberland answered in a private letter to his chief, Madrid, August 24, 1780: "I think it more respectfull in this private matter to inform Your Lordship, that altho' it be true that my friend Mr. Hussey shewd me Count floridablanca's paper of remarks in his own hand-writing; yet I rather strain'd a point in communicating them to Your Lordship and I pledge myself to Your Lordship that if I had moved him on the *Idea* of sending home a Copy, I coud not have fallen upon any measure that would have revolted him more: or given him higher matter of offence. I beg to apply this in Answer to an Observation stated in Your public Letter." R.O., S.P.F., Series 94, Vol. 209, pp. 202, 203.

sey's promises. Providing he understood this document fully and truly he should have immediately left Spain.

Cumberland seems not to have understood the document fully and truly. He wrote to Hillsborough in his first dispatch from Aranjuez: "Not a moment was lost by Mr. Hussey upon our meeting in assuring me by the Minister's authority, that no article touching the cession of Gibraltar or Minorca would be obtruded, *either in the preliminaries or final treaty*;[10] that, upon this declaration, he had consented to use the Minister's own words in his letters[11] to Your Lordship and me, trusting that I should comprehend the implications in his memorandum, and the verbal message he had sent me by his servant Daly."

Now here is a piece of suggestion worthy of Hussey's real genius. Precisely what was the memorandum referred to? The memorandum of directions for travel sent to Cumberland by Hussey from Aranjuez, to help him on his journey to Spain, that memorandum the implications of which Cumberland had so eagerly seized hold of to justify his journey to Aranjuez in defiance of his instructions? Or was it the more significant, the more explicit memorandum which we have recapitulated and quoted, which Hussey had just displayed in oral translation to Cumberland, explaining that it had been penned by Floridablanca himself? The implications of the former in reference to the Spanish Minister's pledge might have satisfied Cumberland that Floridablanca had

---

[10] Italics inserted. Of course Floridablanca intended to insert these articles not in the preliminaries, nor indeed in the final treaty, but in the secret treaty of exchange which was to accompany the public final treaty, and on which the final treaty was to depend.

[11] Hussey's letters of May 30, 1780, *op. cit.*, which had been modeled on an outline furnished by Floridablanca. AHN, *Est.* 4220, *Expdte.* 2, Docs. 152, 153.

agreed not to bring up the forbidden issues. But the statements of the political memorandum, taken *in juxtaposition* with Hussey's representation of Floridablanca's explicit statement that Gibraltar and Minorca would not be mentioned "either in the preliminaries or the final treaty," can mean only one thing. Floridablanca meant, and Hussey knew that Floridablanca meant, that they should be included in the secret treaty of exchange which was to be negotiated under cover of a final public treaty. But Hussey made Cumberland believe that all was well, that neither Gibraltar nor the American Colonies would come on the carpet.

Cumberland cheerfully accepted these thaumaturgical assurances. To the eagerly believing playwright the political memorandum signified exactly the opposite of its actual purport. It meant nothing less than that Spain would really make a separate peace. To him it merely showed *"the difficulties Spain is under for a pretext to separate from her Alliance with france. . . .* These difficulties once removed I have reason to believe there would remain no obstacle to a separate peace, which might not be accommodated to a mutual Satisfaction. . . . The Minister will not state anything as his own proposition, for the reasons abovementioned [i.e., professed reluctance to give umbrage to England]; but his meaning, as convey'd to me, is, that if Great Britain will hold forth Ouvertures to her Colonies for the purpose of removing the occasion of the war, and in case France shall not thereupon withdraw from her American Alliance, which Spain professes to reprobate, Spain will avow her treaty with Great Britain, and, availing herself of this pretext of withdrawing from the war, come into terms for a separate peace.

"This, my Lord, is in substance the idea suggested as

a Satisfaction to the punctilio of His Catholic Majesty.

"The moment for detaching Spain is now as favourable as ever; She is still upon the worst terms with France: Not only the King of Naples but the Queen of Portugal has written pressingly to His Catholic Majesty to make peace with England."[12]

The Englishman was like putty in the hands of this priest. Nor did Hillsborough himself, judging from Cumberland's accounts of his mission, disapprove his decision, against the literal terms of his instructions, to leave Portugal.[13]

As soon as Floridablanca was out of bed Hussey told him of Cumberland's arrival. An interview was arranged for the next day. Cumberland meanwhile on the 19th of June drew up a reply to Floridablanca's unsigned political memorandum, the English sense of which had been conveyed to him by Hussey the day before. The text of this reply was not enclosed by Cumberland in his dispatches, nor is it to be found in the Spanish archives.[14]

All we know about it is from Cumberland's unsatisfying description of it to Hillsborough, which shows us that his idea gained from Hussey's English rendition, the previous day, of Floridablanca's political memoran-

12 Cumberland to Hillsborough, No. 3, Aranjuez, June 26, 1780, R.O., S.P.F., Series 94, Vol. 209, pp. 73-74. For full text see Appendix No. 9.

13 "Mr. Hussey's verbal message to you by the courier he sent to Lisbon in my opinion authorized your undertaking the journey to Spain, for though it did not expressly declare to you that the cession of Gibraltar or Minorca would not be proposed as the basis of a treaty, yet it could admit of no other interpretation." Hillsborough to Hussey, by Daly, St. James's, August 4, 1780, R.O., S.P.F., Series 94, Vol. 209, p. 158.

14 "Mr. Cumberland thought proper to make a reply, but has not sent copy of his reply or of the Count's paper of observations. The Reply was delivered to the Count by Mr. Hussey on the 19th of June in the morning, and in the evening of the same day Mr. Cumberland had his Audience of the Spanish Minister to whom he delivered Lord Hillsborough's Letter of the 17th of April. . . ." *Précis* of Cumberland's correspondence to October 14, 1780, R.O., S.P.F., Series 94, Vol. 254, p. 329 *verso*.

dum, was that of an express assurance that Gibraltar, at least, would not be touched upon. "My Instructions being peremptory against entering into discussion of any Propositions tending to terms of reconciliation between the King and his Colonies, or between Great Britain and France, I form'd my Reply to the paper of observations in conformity thereto, and in the morning of the nineteenth Mr. Hussey carried it to the Minister: The said paper containing an avow'd acquiescence [so Cumberland had been persuaded] as to the points of Gibraltar and Minorca, I signified my readiness to wait upon the Minister according to his appointment, and in the evening by Mr. Hussey's introduction had the honor of paying my respects."[15] The meeting that evening was little more than a polite if lengthy exchange of civilities during the course of which Cumberland delivered Hillsborough's letter of introduction, which also constituted his powers for these conversations. Another conference was arranged for two days later, and it was Cumberland's understanding that the English-speaking secretary, Campo, would be present, and that an attempt would then be made to reduce to writing the thoughts of both parties on peace.

Before the meeting took place news reached Madrid of the Lord George Gordon riots in London which began June 2, 1780. For several days a mob under the leadership of the anti-Catholic fanatic, Lord George Gordon, had surged through the city, assaulting and burning, and for a brief space of time threatened to control the capital and the government. Doubtless the first news was exaggerated,—in a few days news arrived from Aranda, at Paris, that the riots were under control and the leaders

[15] By the "paper of observations" Cumberland means Floridablanca's unsigned political memorandum.

apprehended. But the event had its effect on the first real business interview of Cumberland. To his consternation, Campo was not there, nor were any materials for writing observable. Floridablanca began by glibly expressing his condolences for the terrible events in London. Cumberland, his heart in his throat, replied that they would have the result of uniting the people more firmly than ever behind the existing government. Floridablanca then went on to explain the sincere desire of the King of Spain for a separate peace with England. "Find an Expedient only to satisfy His Catholic Majesty as to his Engagements with France, and Spain will make it a salvo for treating separately with Great Britain," he exclaimed to Cumberland, and he added that with respect to America, Spain to this hour had resisted every idea of a treaty. He went so far as to speak disapprovingly of France's American engagements, and pledged his word of honor that no means were used by Spain for fomenting the American revolt.

Cumberland's detailed account of the interview does not disagree very much with the summary made in a note by Floridablanca on the day of the meeting. "I told him," he wrote for reference, "that without resolving on a means of treating with the first [France] in order to save its engagements all the rest of the edifice would be built on sand."[16]

---

[16] "Mr. Cumberland told me that the personal desires of His Britannic Majesty were to negotiate for peace, and that they would not vary from these; even though the Ministry may change, they would parley. That it was a matter of speaking on the basis of the treaty of Paris with the additions, modifications, and declarations which should appear desirable. That they would proceed with Spain the same way that in the said treaty of Paris they had proceeded with France [in 1763]; that in order to see a way of satisfying France and her engagements with the Colonies, which is the first and principal difficulty I put to him, he would reflect upon it and

In another conference on the following day, June 22, Floridablanca, according to the Englishman, asked him to submit his thoughts in writing, and stated that at this particular crisis of things in London he would prefer Cumberland to accommodate him in waiting for the issue there.[17]

News that the riots had been quelled reached the Court the next day, and Cumberland heard of it, though not immediately from Floridablanca or Campo. He therefore composed some reflections on the present difficulties between England and Spain, ascribing them in the main to the irresponsible precipitancy of France in making an alliance with the American Colonies without even consulting Spain. Since France had taken secret steps to make a separate peace with England in 1763, so now Spain would be perfectly honorable in doing the same without consulting her ally, particularly because Spain and France found themselves at war with England for absolutely different reasons, and Spain had refrained from any obligations with the revolted Colonies of England. He then submitted some propositions for an armistice, mutual surrender of prisoners, etc., for a peace on the basis of the treaty of Paris: "It rests now with the Court of Spain to approve her sincerity and meet G. Britain in the overture she has made: If she wishes to have a mutual restitution of Conquests, it is

make some notes which he would send me in order to hear mine, and be able to send some account to his Court of the beginning of negotiation.

"He excused himself also from speaking about France for various reasons of consequence; and we did not pass on to any point of interest of France and Spain, because I said that without resolving on a mode of treating with the former and saving her engagements, everything else would be building on sand." Minutes of first conference with Cumberland, Wednesday, June 21, 1780, AHN, *Est.* 4220, *Expdte.* 2, Doc. 163.

[17] Cumberland's No. 3 to Hillsborough. See Appendix No. 9. Observe that Floridablanca's note ascribes to Cumberland himself the initiative in the matter of setting down thoughts on paper, in the interview of June 21.

offered to her; If she prefers to abide by mutual acqui-
sitions G. Britain will accommodate to her desires;[18] If
she goes still further, and wishes for an exchange of
possessions, (*with the reservations previously explained,*
[i.e., the Gibraltar and Minorca reservations]) the Minister will be pleas'd to signify what his Requisitions are;
and Mr. Cumberland will candidly and respectfully give
him his Opinion in the case."[19]

The astute Floridablanca had now easily led Cumberland into a familiar misstep of the inexperienced diplomatist, that of putting something on paper without
having previously secured any expression in writing
from his adversary. Cumberland made things worse by
describing his paper in so many words as "British overtures." For this he received his first reproof from Hillsborough, as well as an expression of disappointment
from his friend and patron, Lord George Germain.[20]
Both were particularly concerned, too, that Cumberland
had not sent home a copy of the articles submitted.[21]

[18] News of the capture of Mobile by the forces of Bernardo Galvez was
published in the *Gaceta de Madrid,* supplementary issue of June 23, 1780,
a copy of which was enclosed by Cumberland to Hillsborough, presumably
in his No. 2 of June 30.

[19] A Spanish text in Hussey's handwriting, entitled "Cumberland's Dis-
courses and Reflexions on the Way of Establishing Peace without the Intervention of France," is in AHN, *Est.* 4220, *Expdte.* 2, Doc. 165, dated
Aranjuez, June 25, 1780. It is a translation, slightly abridged, of the English original in R.O., S.P.F., Series 94, Vol. 209, pp. 87-89. The Spanish text
of the proposed treaty articles corresponds to the first six pages of the
outline of a proposed treaty which is filed together with Cumberland's
instructions in *ibid.,* Vol. 254, *ff.,* discussed above in connection with Cumberland's instructions. A draft by Floridablanca for a letter to Fernan
Nuñez directed that "Cumberland's famous reflexions" be enclosed. AHN,
Est. 4220, *Expdte.* 2, Doc. 17.

[20] Hillsborough to Cumberland, by Daly, St. James's, August 4, 1780,
R.O., S.P.F., Series 94, Vol. 209, pp. 158-163; Germain to Cumberland,
Stoneland Lodge, July 29, 1780, *Stopford-Sackville Papers,* I, 334.

[21] As already stated the articles were altogether innocuous and conventional. They revealed no British terms.

Even now Floridablanca evaded writing down any terms in reply to Cumberland. He sent Campo to say that the Minister refrained from suggesting any expedient for the "salvo" because he did not want to cause umbrage to the Court of Great Britain; already Spain had gotten into two wars by attempting to mediate in the disputes of Great Britain. Campo delivered, however, an autograph letter of Floridablanca for Lord Hillsborough. After polite expressions of Spain's desire for peace, it stated the requirement for ending the war: "the necessity of finding a road that may lead us to the end of the Negotiation without the King's failing in his engagements with the Most Christian King his nephew; engagements into which, exclusive of those of long standing, the calamity of war forced him to enter." If Cumberland should receive instructions to this effect Floridablanca would be glad to facilitate the course of the business. The note delivered, Campo and some other gentlemen of the Court helped Cumberland, immensely impressed by these courtesies, into his coach as he set out at midnight for Madrid, whither the Spanish Court was now again on the move.[22]

[22] Floridablanca to Lord Hillsborough, Aranjuez, June 26, 1780, R.O., S.P.F., Series 94, Vol. 209, pp. 91-94. See also Cumberland's No. 2, *op. cit.*

"I am handing you the letter which by His Majesty's orders I am writing to Lord Hillsborough, which goes unsealed in order that Mr. Cumberland may be informed of it. I have not advised that the negotiation be suspended on account of the riot,—that is a matter of indifference to us,—and we would rather follow it up promptly; but I suspect that this gentleman does not have the powers to overcome my first objection, which concerns the means of safeguarding the obligation [*de salvar los Empeños*], of France; for all his reflexions aim at proving that we can make a separate peace, following the example of France in the last war. At that time France did pursue a separate negotiation, but did not make a special and separate peace. In the negotiation France dealt with Spanish interests such as the restitution of Havana and the Philippines. In these terms we can treat now or it will be necessary to find some other decent and acceptable means. If this gentleman holds instructions for it, we will talk; if not, he ought

The letter to Hillsborough was hurried to London in the hands of Hussey's servant, the man Daly, courier extraordinary in all of these comings and goings between London, Lisbon and Madrid, and of course the confidant of his master and thus of Floridablanca himself. Cumberland settled down in Madrid impatiently awaiting an answer.

"On the Return, which the wisdom of Your Lordship and the rest of His Majesty's Ministers shall make to this Report," he wrote to his chief, "depends the issue of the Negotiation. If His Majesty shall be advised to cause some declaration to be made of his gracious disposition towards a reconcilement with his deluded Subjects in rebellion; and if this be communicated from your lordship to Count floridablanca immediately, or mediately by empowering Me to that effect; and if this be done in mild and friendly terms towards Spain, who stipulates nothing, but submits the whole to Great Britain, requesting it only as a Saving for her punctilio, I think I have strong grounds to say her family Compact will no longer hold her from a separate Peace with G. Britain A great event will then take place in Europe, and a signal honour accrue to Your Lordship's administration: Zealously imploring Providence to guide your Councils for the best,

to ask for them, or take such steps as may best conform to his orders. In the intelligence which you have at your disposal you are already informed of our way of thinking. I have only to add that if you want to get back the papers which you delivered to me they will be returned; they contain nothing of substance nor do we want to compromise anybody." [Floridablanca] to Hussey, undated, but presumably June 25, 1780, AHN, *Est.* 4220, *Expdte.* 2, Doc. 117.

The reference to the return of the papers is apparently to observations and draft articles which Cumberland through Hussey had placed in Floridablanca's hands.

I wait this determination with anxious expectation."[23]

At home Cumberland had not been accustomed to
have signal attentions heaped on him. At Aranjuez and
at Madrid and later at the Escorial and at La Granja,
as the year wore on, he and his family received in his
capacity as an agent of the British King many of those
courtesies which only Spaniards can enact with such
perfect assiduity. He was shown through the Palace at
Aranjuez, was offered a fine pointer dog and actually
given a horse, to the jealousy of some of his friends in
the *corps,*—a steed which in his *Memoirs* appears as a
marvelous creature, but in a contemporary document
limps a little with what looks, through the ages, sus-
piciously like a spavin. The King gave him pieces of
marble and granite for a collection which he commenced. Other horses were furnished his family out of
the royal stables, and two particularly handsome Anda-
lusian animals were presented for the British King, and
duly sent en route to England. Cumberland at Hussey's
suggestion—it having been assented to by "the Minister"
—recommended to Hillsborough that some gold muslins
be sent to Madrid as a gift for the Queen of Spain.

Cumberland had two eligible and dashing daughters,
if we are to believe his pardonable descriptions of them.[24]
"When these young Englishwomen," says their father,
"habited in their Spanish dresses, (and attractive, as I

[23] Cumberland's No. 3, Aranjuez, June 26, *op. cit.*

[24] Fanny Burney, who must have been older and less captivating than
they, writing from Brighton the previous year about the Misses Cumberland, said that they were "reckoned the flashers of the place, yet everybody laughs at them for their airs, affectations, tonish graces and imper-
tinences"; and Mrs. Thrale says that they were hissed out of a playhouse
because of the height of their feathers. George Paston (Miss E. M. Sym-
onds), *Little Memoirs of the Eighteenth Century* (London, 1901), 95.

may presume to say they were by the bloom and beauty of their persons) passed through the streets of Madrid, their coach was brought to frequent stops, and hardly found its passage through the crowd."[25] The Princess of Asturias gave the daughters and their mother a private audience, so Cumberland recorded, even condescended to take a pattern of their riding habits, and gazed curiously on their jewelry. Truly, no greater honors were ever to be heaped upon the house of Cumberland than this supreme tribute! Soon all Madrid was in English women's riding togs. The playwright admired pictures, went to the theater to hear a celebrated tragedienne, dabbled with Latin manuscripts at the Escorial. Had he not broken his arm and had a painful time mending it, this adventure to Spain so far would have been perfect felicity, for it gave him all the attentions and all the caterings which he had previously seen bestowed only on those lordly personages who in England were his patrons, whose world to him was heaven itself. He became the intimate friend of the Austrian Ambassador, Count Joseph de Kaunitz, who wooed his elder daughter; and another illustrious young Austrian, General Pallavicini, a military *attaché* at the legation in Madrid, successively and unsuccessfully laid siege to the hand of first one and then the other of these tantalizing creatures.[26]

[25] *Memoirs, op. cit.,* 93.

[26] In his *Memoirs,* II, 98, Cumberland delicately suggests that poor young Kaunitz, one of the four sons of the illustrious diplomatist Prince Kaunitz, really died of unrequited love. Presumably this was Joseph de Kaunitz who was not of a robust constitution. He was Austrian Minister to Spain, from May 1780 to January 1785. He died on a voyage to Italy, in February 1785. He had succeeded his brother Dominic at the Court of Spain. See D'Arneth et Flammermont, *Correspondance Secrète de Mercy-Argenteau avec l'Empereur Joseph II et le Prince de Kaunitz,* I, 46, note 1. Pallavicini

But we are anticipating, in glancing ahead at the life of the Cumberlands in Spain, straying aside from the strictly diplomatic phases of his mission, and suggesting that after all it did not come to a speedy head. Beginning this round of new and delectable experiences by no means dulled the anxiety with which Cumberland awaited word from Hillsborough. Soon after the Spanish Foreign Minister returned to Madrid from Aranjuez, some more communications and conferences followed, during the month of July.

News had arrived at Madrid of the capitulation of Charleston, South Carolina, to General Sir Henry Clinton, an event which Cumberland believed had duly impressed the Spanish Court, though they nevertheless might hold out for better peace terms in the actual negotiations until the end of hopes founded on the departure from Cadiz on July 31 of the great Franco-Spanish fleet. The first Madrid conference occurred soon after the news from Charleston. Floridablanca congratulated Cumberland on the happy event for His Britannic Majesty's arms: "He observed there were some who affected to talk down our successes in America, but for his part he saw them in their full light, and hop'd they woud be follow'd by the total Submission or reduction of the Colonies; that then there woud be no

later in the eastern wars had his head sabered clean off by a Turkish soldier.

Joseph de Kaunitz's dispatches show that he made good use of his acquaintance with the Cumberlands, including the "zweien artigen Töchtern," to apprise his father, Prince Kaunitz, of the latest developments of Cumberland's mission, information highly useful to the Austrian Chancellor's plans for mediation. See *Haus-, Hof-, und Staatsarchiv*, Vienna, *Spanien, Korrespondenz*, Fascicles 140, 141, 142, and 143. For a typical dispatch exhibiting his close contact with Cumberland, see Count J. de Kaunitz to Prince Kaunitz, No. 6, Madrid, January 22, 1781, *ibid.*, Fascicle 143, Vol. 37. I am indebted to Dr. Fritz Reinöhl of Vienna for selecting for me the relevant documents out of this series.

difficulties to adjust between us; he felt the force of what I had said respecting a communication of our ideas on the subject of the Salvo,[27] and told me he woud talk with His Catholic Majesty upon it." Floridablanca agreed that if Hillsborough's letter should not be specific as to satisfying Spanish engagements with France but should nevertheless be "couch'd in mild and friendly terms . . . he will nevertheless receive it in good part and concurr with me in suggesting some expedient for this purpose, by which the only obstacle to a sincere and separate accommodation with Great Britain may be removed." It was at this same conference that Floridablanca told Cumberland that he *"might assure his Court, Spain would never acknowledge the Independence of the revolted Colonies, untill it was admitted by Great Britain."*[28]

Floridablanca had held up to Cumberland and to the British Ministry the horrendous spectacle of an American envoy stalking the Spanish Court about Castile trying to snare it into an American alliance. Another device was now brought forth to do equally good service. It worked like a charm. Campo wrote a note to Cumberland to say that the Spanish *chargé* at St. Petersburg had been approached by Catherine II's Government about a possible Russian mediation. Cumberland rose to the fly. He saw his own importance as a peacemaker endangered by such an outside instrument, and immediately wrote from Madrid back to Campo (at San Ilde-

---

[27] Cumberland had suggested that while waiting for an answer from Hillsborough they might informally discuss various formulas which might serve as a "salvo" for Spain's obligations to France, since Floridablanca had hesitated to construct one and Cumberland had feared Hillsborough would find little to go on in the rather general and vague intimations of the Spanish Minister's letter to him.

[28] Cumberland to Hillsborough, No. 6, Madrid, July 21, 1780, R.O., S.P.F., Series 94, Vol. 209, pp. 124-125. Italics inserted.

fonso) to ask whether the mediation offer were confined
to Great Britain and Spain only, or extended to France
as well, and where the proposed place of negotiation.
Campo replied from San Ildefonso that he lacked these
particulars. "We haven't given, nor shall give any
answer before hearing from your Court," he hastened to
reassure him, and persuaded the eager playwright not
to leave his wife and follow the regular diplomatic corps
to San Ildefonso to hold further talk about this mediation proposal. "Your unexpected visit will make too
much noise here as it was generaly spread you staid at
Madrid on account of the Lady's actual disposition."
And the perspicacious Campo noted for his chief's attention: "Stupid Cumberland with his fantastic genius has
become uneasy about the Russian business, thinking
already his coming negotiation is about to expire."[29]
With some satisfaction and emphasis Cumberland re-
layed Campo's reassurance to London.

There can be no doubt that Floridablanca's remark
that Spain would not recognize the independence of the
American Colonies until Great Britain did so, was
thoroughly consonant with real Spanish policy; but it
was putting it a bit strong when the Foreign Minister

[29] Cumberland to Campo, Madrid, July 23 and 24, and Campo to Cumberland, San Ildefonso, July 22, and 24, 1780; Memorandum of Campo for
Floridablanca, July 23 or 24, 1780; AHN, *Est.* 4220, *Expdte.* 2, Docs. 168,
169, 171, 172, 173; Cumberland to Hillsborough, No. 4, Madrid, July 4,
1780, R.O., S.P.F., Series 94, Vol. 209, p. 115. To his chagrin, Cumberland
later discovered, by means of an alleged intercepted dispatch, that no
Russian mediation offer was made to Spain until December 1780. Cumberland to Hillsborough, No. 18, Madrid, January 3, 1781, F.O., 72, I, 1. In
his memoir to Shelburne of 1782, Br. Museum, *Additional MSS*, 28851, he
explains that he received a copy of the intercepted dispatch (Floridablanca
to P. Normande, Spanish *chargé* at St. Petersburg, December 23, 1780),
and other relevant documents, from the Danish ex-Consul General at
Madrid, who, footloose, professed to be seeking a place in British service.
The Russian mediation and Spanish diplomacy may be followed in Dánvila,
op. cit. V, 344-350. See note at end of Chapter I, above.

stated that he would be glad enough to see the Colonies
subjugated if that would result in clearing the road to
peace by the removal of the difficulty of France's pledge
to them. For if Great Britain were unembarrassed in
America she could then turn the strength of her arms to
the reconquest of Florida and the relief of Gibraltar.
Spanish repossession of Gibraltar depended on the
continued involvement of British naval forces in the
new world. A stalemate would have been more propitious for the accomplishment of Spanish purposes in
that theater.

Nothing went on in all his conversations at the Spanish Court to which Hussey was not privy, so reported
Cumberland. Literally as well as figuratively the priest
served as his right-hand man, for he actually wrote, at
Cumberland's dictation, the text of some of his dispatches, taking copies of course for Floridablanca. "My
excellent friend Mr. Hussey," Cumberland described
him, "who rises every hour in my esteem, whose attachment to his natural Sovereign is such, that I am fre-
quently compell'd to moderate its ardour, lest I shoud
forfeit the advantages of preserving him still in the
character of a middle man; with his assistance I have no
doubt of executing your Instructions with a Success,
that will derive it's chief credit from his labours."[30]
Hillsborough ironically approved of the lively assistance of "good Mr. Hussey" and hoped that it might
make Floridablanca see the light.[31] Hussey on his side
preserved the fiction of a middleman, and complained to
Germain that the Spanish Court was inattentive to him

[30] Cumberland to Hillsborough, No. 4, Madrid, July 4, 1780; No. 12, Madrid, September 24, 1780; *ibid.* p. 115, 211.
[31] Hillsborough to Cumberland, St. James's, August 4, 1780, R.O., S.P.F.,
Series 94, Vol. 209, p. 165.

because of his intimacy with Cumberland![32] He added
a touch to his rôle by supplying Cumberland and the
British Ministry with some trivial Spanish naval and
military information.

Hillsborough dated his reply August 3, 1780, and sent
it back to Spain by the faithful (to Hussey) Daly. But
before it could reach the Spanish Court the greatest
maritime disaster of the war overtook the British merchant marine. In the early morning of the 9th of August,
while moving two to three hundred miles off Cape St.
Vincent, the joint Franco-Spanish fleet under Córdoba
luckily came upon a great fleet of English merchant
ships en route for the East and West India stations,
with vast stores of munitions and provisions worth a mil-
lion and a half sterling. The rich armada had just been
released, prematurely, from protection of the major
units of its convoy, and had not separated for its
respective destinations. The happy Spaniards and
Frenchmen rounded up fifty-five of the sixty-three vessels in the fleet and took them, their numerous crews,
and a smaller number of transport troops, triumphantly
in to Cadiz.[33] The armament which had set out from
that port on the 31st of July had thus justified expectations. British victories in Carolina were more than
balanced by this achievement. At about the same time
news reached Spain of the interception of the big
Quebec convoy off the Gulf of St. Lawrence by Franco-
American forces. Mobile also was under Spanish colors,
and British settlements on the Honduran coast contained. Aside from the financial strain of the war, Spain

[32] Hussey to Lord George Germain, Madrid, September 1, 1780, Stopford-Sackville Papers, I, 337.
[33] A. T. Mahan, Major Operations of the Navies in the War of American Independence, 157; Dánvila y Collado, Reinado de Carlos III, V, 110,
gives fifty-two prizes, £1,500,000 cargo, and 3144 prisoners.

stood in little real danger anywhere and was free to turn
her energies to the besieging of Gibraltar. A joint
Franco-Spanish expedition against that fortress, under
the command of Admiral d'Estaing, was planned.
Hillsborough's answer therefore reached Madrid at a
rare hour of Spanish triumph, when there was least
need for any immediate and separate peace with Great
Britain, and the greatest hope for still more glorious
victories.

At no moment before the final fall of the North Ministry did George III ever waver in his position. He
would not accept the idea of independence, explicit or
tacit, under any guise or dress. He could not see that
under the Floridablanca formula of a "middle-term" as
a "salvo," the fateful European diplomatic combination
abetted by Vergennes, which was pressing Great Britain
to her knees, might be broken up. He would not see that
under the guise of a truce and of dependence masked as
"tacit independence," and based on the military *status
quo* in America, France might be eased out of the war
by Spanish pressure, and the Family Alliance broken
up forever,—always at the cost of Gibraltar. Even then,
in that gloomy month of August,[34] he was preparing to
dissolve the Parliament, now six years old and increas-
ingly restive under the burden of multiplying disasters
and the growing influence of the Opposition, and to
strengthen his majority by royal corruption at the
polls,—an end abundantly achieved in the general elec-
tion of October 1780. Hillsborough, who had conducted
the Spanish correspondence, was a thorough disciple of
the royal policy. He received his appointment because
of the correctness and consistency of his American sentiments. It was Hillsborough who had made the celebrated

[34] Trevelyan, *George the Third and Charles James Fox*, II, 314.

speech in the House of Lords, on March 5, 1778, at the second reading of the American conciliatory bill that had established the unsuccessful Carlisle peace negotiation. Passionately denouncing the bill, he had declared that it marked the most disgraceful day his country had ever seen.[35] Germain, under whose protecting wing the Hussey negotiations had commenced, was of similar political stripe. Further, there had just arrived from France an extraordinary secret letter from the French Premier, Maurepas, which seemed to indicate that France might be considering peace—a letter which we do not have in text, but which reflected the worry which the Spanish negotiations and the general financial strain of the war was causing to the French Government. These elements in the situation will be more properly considered in the next chapter, but the Maurepas letter, whatever it said, convinced the King at this time that France had some weighty reason to wish for peace, "which makes me a little more hopeful that Spain is resolved to end the war, and that M. de Maurepas must also do the same."[36] The obstinate English monarch refused to unbend. Hillsborough's reply to Floridablanca, placed before the King on the 2nd of August,[37] went out with the monarch's emphatic approval. The royal correspondence is full of a determination not to allow the American Colonies to be mentioned in any shape or form, during any negotiations with the European enemies of his Empire.[38]

Stripped of polite expressions and professions, the Hillsborough note simply said that Great Britain was unaware of the engagements which existed between

[35] *Parliamentary History*, XIX, 842-843.

[36] George III to Lord North, Windsor Castle, July 30, 1780, Donne, *Correspondence of King George the Third*, V, 103, 105.

[37] *ibid.*, V, 105.

[38] *ibid., passim.*

Spain and France, and in ignorance of their terms did not feel competent to point out any such "road" as Floridablanca had suggested as the way to peace. Hillsborough professed not to suppose that these engagements could have any relation to the state of the King's rebellious subjects in America. Spain, unlike France, had not engaged in the war because of this "unnatural rebellion," but had reprobated the unjustifiable measures of the French in regard to British America. "From the beginning of this Revolt," Hillsborough reminded the Spanish Minister, "the King's repeated Declarations have evinced His Parental Sentiments towards his rebellious Subjects, and the Clemency with which He has treated those Colonies which have come back to their Allegiance carries a convincing Proof of His gracious Intentions to receive into His Peace and Protection All those who, sensible of their former Errors shall return to their Duty as Subjects to His Majesty, and to their legal and Constitutional Dependance on the Crown of Great Britain. . . . If the Information that I have presumed to give your Excellency of the King's Conduct and Intentions with regard to His Subjects in Rebellion shall by any means tend to the opening of that Road to Negotiation. . . . I shall be happy to have taken up so large a portion of your time. . . ."[39]

Cumberland was empowered to draw up and hasten to England the project of a treaty with Spain, providing that the expressions of Hillsborough's reply should open the "road" down which the Spanish Foreign Minister might be prepared to travel.[40]

[39] The original copy of this letter, in the Spanish archives, AHN, *Est.* 4220, *Expdte.* 2, Doc. 177, is dated August 3, as are also the copies in Spanish translation in Hussey's (Doc. 175) and Campo's (Doc. 176) handwriting. The copy in R.O., S.P.F., Series 94, Vol. 209, p. 154, is dated August 4.

[40] Hillsborough to Cumberland, St. James's, August 4, 1780, R.O., S.P.F., Series 94, Vol. 209, p. 158.

CHAPTER VI

GIBRALTAR, AND THE "MIDDLE ROAD"

CUMBERLAND, as soon as the ubiquitous Daly arrived at Madrid with the dispatches from London, hastened across the mountains to present Hillsborough's answer to Floridablanca at the palace of La Granja. There at San Ildefonso the Court was loitering in the cool fastnesses of the Guadarramas, where the fountains quietly played in the agreeable shade of great horsechestnut trees under the interminable murmur of their innumerable bees. At La Granja, Castile seemed a serene and tranquil world far distant from the clashing thunders of West Indian battlefleets. Others also had hastened to San Ildefonso. Particularly Count d'Estaing, as the special envoy of France, with renewed plans for Franco-Spanish military and naval action, calculated to stiffen the Spanish Court against supposed British blandishments, and to hold forth to Spain the reasonable certainty of the glorious capture of Gibraltar by immediate joint endeavor that very year under the leadership of d'Estaing himself. Jay, the American, was there, too. The diplomatic corps was busy with guesses what it was all about.[1]

Cumberland delivered Hillsborough's reply on the evening of August 31, 1780. At that conference with Floridablanca, a short one, nothing happened to discourage the Englishman. But on the 2nd of September another meeting occurred, in which it was apparent that the Minister found nothing acceptable in what Hills-

[1] Francesco Pesaro (Venetian Ambassador) to the Senate, No. 213, San Ildefonso, September 5, 1780, *Archivio di Stato* (Venice), *Dispacci, Spagna*, filza 180. See also No. 216 of September 24, *ibid.*

borough had conveyed. He began by stressing Spanish commitments to France, an ally never to be deserted.

He said: "To all inquiries, which France has made through her Ambassador touching your visit in Spain, I have answered that the King of Spain would be faithful to his engagements, and have divulged nothing further of the business."

He then observed that the British Court had given no answer to the earlier articles which had been transmitted through Hussey before Cumberland's arrival in Spain, that is to say, the Johnstone articles.

"Those articles," observed Cumberland, "were formed upon the vague suggestions of Mr. Johnstone, which were absolutely unwarranted and solemnly disavowed by my Court."

"Admitting this," retorted Floridablanca, "I see no reason why his articles might not be considered, though the overtures on which they were founded were disavowed, seeing that I spoke the sentiments of my Court, even though Mr. Johnstone might not convey those of Great Britain. It seems to me surprising, by the way, that such presumption in a subject should pass unnoticed by any mark of the royal displeasure."

"Do you mean," asked Cumberland, astonished, "to found the propositions of Spain upon the substance of the Paper which you committed to Mr. Hussey?"

"I do," replied the Minister, with some hesitation.

"Then how can you now make mention of the Gibraltar article, which stands as one of those particulars, after the assurances made before and since my departure from Lisbon?" reproachfully inquired the nonplussed Cumberland.

"We cannot require that now," said Floridablanca imperturbably, after some allusion to future pretentions to Gibraltar and the security it would give to a general peace, "but one inadmissible article need not preclude an answer to the rest."[2]

Alarmed at this statement and remembering enough about the original paper which Hussey had brought to London to realize that it contained things to which he could not possibly agree, Cumberland quit the subject, and decided to consult the various documents which Hussey had with him. He thought that Hussey kept papers which had committed Floridablanca further than that minister would now allow. "As the possession of those papers gave Mr. Hussey greater advantage over him [Floridablanca], than the referring to them gave me, with other obvious reasons, it appeared the wisest way to get him into the Conferences, which now went upon ground forbidden by my Instructions, and from which he [Hussey] had been excluded, as knowing him possest of vouchers, that spoke a language very different from what they found it now convenient to adopt." At least such was the account of the interview which Cumberland returned to Hillsborough.[3]

[2] Cumberland to Hillsborough, No. 12, Madrid, September 24, 1780, R.O., S.P.F., Series 94, Vol. 209, p. 211.

[3] Cumberland to Hillsborough, No. 12, Madrid, September 24, 1780, R.O., S.P.F., Series 94, Vol 209, p. 211. I have presumed to put the above conversation out of Cumberland's dispatch into direct discourse, adhering rigidly to the text, but placing my own interpretations on the feelings of the speakers. It is desirable here to reproduce the account of the San Ildefonso interviews noted down by the English-speaking Campo, who was present:

"Cumberland arrived at S. Ildefonso on the 31st of August and that night had a conference with the Honorable Count Floridablanca at which I was present. He delivered the enclosed letter from Lord Hillsborough full of expressions of cordiality, compliments and good words, etc., in which nothing is offered relative to the peace. Three days later he had another conference with His Excellency, at which I was also present, in which His Excellency intimated to him how little the negotiation would advance if

The particular papers proved to be in Hussey's strong box with his London bankers. Campo, wishing to refresh his memory by reference to them, had already asked Hussey in vain to present them.[4] The perturbed Cumberland returned to Madrid and held a long talk with Hussey. It was finally resolved that Hussey should now go to San Ildefonso and enter into further discussions; for Cumberland had the entertaining theory that the Spanish Minister, who had never put his name to any papers except those of March 1780, in which Gibraltar was a *sine qua non,* had over-extended himself to the good priest! Hussey accordingly went. He sent back this word, the text of which we have significantly enough from the Spanish archives, not from the English. After stating that Floridablanca had explained that his engagements with France were nothing more than the usual agreement not to make a separate peace, he wrote:

"As for getting any proposition from him to be laid before the Cabinet, it is in vain to attempt it. He refers to what the Court of G. Britain knows already of the requisitions of Spain. And altho the propositions of Mr. Johnstone be disavowed by G. Britain & declared unauthorised, yet he says the mind of Spain is plainly seen thro the marginal *answers* given to them. As moreover G. Britain already knows the wishes of Spain, thro me, on the

things went on as they had until now, and what a great mistake it was for his Ministry to pursue such a policy.

"The next day he had another individual conference with me, to which His Excellency had agreed, and finally he returned to Madrid on the fourth of September, offering to write from there some notes to the paper of articles which in the month of January we had remitted by Padre Hussey." AHN, *Est.* 4220, *Expdte.* 2, Doc. 179.

[4] Hussey to Campo, Madrid, September 2, 4, 1780; Campo to Hussey, San Ildefonso, September 3, 1780, AHN, *Est.* 4220, *Expdte.* 2, Docs. 120, 122, 180.

articles of West Florida, Bay of Honduras: & Campeche, She can easily see what must be settled towards a pacification."

Floridablanca regarded efforts to elicit a formal statement from Spain only as attempts to get some damaging declaration to put before France to the ruin of Spain.

"He says you refuse to hear France mention'd or to transmit to G. Britain any general declaration regarding her. . . . I told his Ex:y . . . that I did not know of any articles which you were expressly forbidden to transmit to GB. but those relating to Gibraltar, and Minorca, and the B Colonies in America. The Spanish Minister says also that nothing can be settled here, until the answer of G Britain to the Mediation of Russia comes, which he supposes will be in a few days; but is however of opinion that the result of his Conversation with me should be transmitted with^t delay to the Court of London. He said in a very emphatic manner that the day you and I leave this Country without settling Matters he would imediately treat with Mr. Jay, and acknowledge him."[5]

Again, watch out for Mr. Jay!

The upshot of the whole unsatisfactory situation, from the point of view of Cumberland, was that Hussey was sent back to London (a journey for which he did not scruple to extract liberal travelling expenses from both the English and Spanish Courts), with dispatches describing the state of affairs, to make orally to the British

[5] Hussey to Cumberland, S. Ildefonso, September 10, 1780, AHN, *Est.* 4220, *Expdte.* 2, Doc. 125. There is also a Spanish translation by Hussey of this copy of his letter to Cumberland. *ibid.,* Doc. 126.

Ministry the disagreeable propositions which the envoy had instructions not to listen to or talk about. Characteristically Floridablanca provided Hussey with another memorandum written out in his own handwriting, unsigned, which Hussey presented in London October 14, 1780, as his own personal report. We refer the reader to the appendix of this volume for the text of this interesting document. Suffice here to say that it finally revealed in no doubtful way that two indispensable things, not to mention the minor settlements, were necessary to end the war. Those were Gibraltar, and the "middle road"—the formula necessary to extricate France from her engagements with the American Colonies. If it had been understood when Cumberland left Lisbon that these objects should not be mentioned in the preliminaries, it had been equally well intended that they should be incorporated in a separate, secret exchange treaty on which the final treaty should depend.[6]

The British Cabinet was now perfectly undeceived on the subject of these wonder-working assurances by which Hussey had lured Cumberland from Lisbon to Aranjuez the previous May. It is said that there was some division in the Cabinet on the subject of Gibraltar. At least the French Government possessed itself of an alleged exchange of letters between Hillsborough and Stormont, written just after the dissolution of Parliament and a few weeks before Hussey's arrival in London, in which Hillsborough proposed that Stormont

[6] "Paper delivered by His Excellency confidentially to Don Thomas Hussey the night of September 21, 1780, when he left for England." AHN, *Est.* 4220, *Expdte.* 2, Docs. 128, 129, 130. See Appendix No. 10. There was one copy in Floridablanca's hand, one in Campo's and one in Hussey's. For Spanish payment of Hussey's expenses see Campo's endorsement on Cumberland to Campo, Madrid, October 7, 1780, AHN, *Est.* 4220, *Expdte.* 2, Doc. 185; for English payment, see "Memorandum of Mr. H's Expences," paid October 27, 1780 (£210/10/00). R.O., S.P.F., Series 94, Vol. 209, p. 221.

change places with him in the Cabinet and prepare the cession of Gibraltar. He stated that the Spanish demands on that point were not unreasonable, but that the public would not stand for such a cession. Stormont refused. "I cannot be asked," he retorted, "to take upon myself the dangerous jobs of your office, any more than those of any other servant of the King."[7] Whatever may have been the varying opinion of individual ministers as to the expediency of letting go Gibraltar amid the mounting calamities of the conflict, neither King nor Cabinet, on the eve of the general elections, would listen to the Spanish terms or the Spanish threats. It was decided in a Cabinet meeting of October 19, 1780, "upon the reading of Mr. Cumberland's last letter and the paper brought over by Mr. Hussey that no further step should be taken in this Business for some time."[8]

After two months' delay a reply was sent back by Hussey in person, who wrote from Lisbon the results of his most recent mission. It was so unsatisfactory that Floridablanca, apparently by prearrangement, refused to let him bring a report to Madrid in person.[9] Hus-

[7] Doniol, IV, 502, note.

[8] *Correspondence of King George the Third,* V, 142.

[9] Hussey to Floridablanca, Lisbon, December 28, 1780; and Floridablanca to Hussey, Pardo, January 20, 1781; AHN, *Est.* 4220, *Expdte.* 2, Docs. 131, 134. For text, see Appendix No. 11. See also, on Hussey in Lisbon at this time, and his return to London for spy service, *ibid.,* Docs. 45, 46, 47, 48, 49, 51, 135, 136, 137, 138, 142, 166, 186, 187, 188.

The essential paragraphs of the original documents printed in the Appendix are herewith given in translation:

Hussey to Floridablanca, Lisbon, December 28, 1780: "After a delay of almost two months, Lord Hillsborough dictated to me the following reply to what I had exposed to him by Your Excellency's orders touching the peace overtures which have passed between the two courts.

"That he [Lord Hillsborough] was very sorry that the matter of Gibraltar had been again touched on after the British Cabinet had declared that Mr. Cumberland's trip to Madrid took place only on condition that there should be no mention of Gibraltar nor of the English Colonies . . .

sey's Spanish masters sent him back to London, where
he was expected to do more effective service as a spy.
For a while he continued in contact with the British
Ministry,[10] but soon things got so hot for him there that
he found it expedient, in September 1781, to move to

that to consider the cession or exchange of Gibraltar as a *sine qua non* of
peace is in effect to break off the negotiation. . . .

"That the Court of London is ignorant of the middle term which the
Spanish Minister suggests should be sought to make peace in order that
neither Spain nor France may appear untrustworthy in this War; and if
Spain hits upon this middle term, Great Britain is persuaded that the
pacific views of that Court will induce it to propose it, being assured of the
most prompt and sincere acceptance on the part of Great Britain. The
middle term of *feudal* dependence which Your Excellency mentioned to me
will not be admitted. . . .

"After dictating to me this reply, Lord Hillsborough entered into further
conversation on the point of Gibraltar, saying that so far as he was concerned it would please him if it were ceded to Spain, but that he would
not dare to advise it to the King, for if the Nation should revolt this advice
might cost him his head. . . ."

Floridablanca to Hussey, Pardo, January 20, 1781: ". . . that Minister
[Hillsborough] and his Court have formed the idea that Gibraltar was not
to be mentioned nor the Colonies, in case of Mr. Cumberland's coming to
Madrid. On this point there is much misunderstanding, because upon our
side it was only agreed that nothing should be said about Gibraltar in the
Preliminaries, but it was proposed, that by a secret convention, or separate
treaty, the cession or exchange of that fortress might be arranged and
effected at the same time as the Preliminaries of Peace. That was uniformly
my language. . . ."

[10] "To-day in conversation with the Secretary of State he said that if
perhaps Spain offers the island of Porto Rico for Gibraltar he did not
doubt arranging it with this Nation. The Secretary of State suggested that
I should write to Your Excellency and that it could be concerted here
secretly. I replied that it was impossible because of the misunderstanding
there had been on this very point. It appeared to me worth while to inform
Your Excellency of this, although I have no faith in it. Nothing new since
my last." Hussey to Floridablanca, London, June 20, 1781, cipher. Floridablanca in August acknowledged this dispatch "treating of the miserable
business which they proposed to you on the exchange of Porto Rico for
Gibraltar. . . . Try to find out the future dispositions of that Government's
squadrons and expeditions, for it always helps us to know about them in
time. Indicate to me if any good way can be discovered by which my dispatches in reply can go safely, because from here all I can do is to take
advantage of the opportunity of some person's going to Paris by chance."
AHN, *Est.* 4220, *Expdte.* 2, Docs. 140, 141.

Belgium. We find him thereafter travelling about Europe, with a wealthy young Catholic *protégé,* an English expatriate, one Jack Webb, under instructions from Jack's father to inculcate into the lad by suggestion a hatred of England and all things English! The Abbé was corresponding with Campo to find a suitable Spanish bride for this prospective Spanish subject, with what success the documents do not reveal.[11] Hussey now passes out of our picture. After the war he returned to his post at the Spanish Embassy in London, was in later years in intimate correspondence with the Irish Catholics, and became Rector of the new Catholic College at Maynooth in Ireland, in 1796, and Bishop of Waterford and Lismore shortly thereafter. It is not within the purview of the present narrative to describe the adventures and intrigues of this ecclesiastic during the Irish troubles of the 'nineties. The athletic prelate, whom Lecky calls the most able English-speaking bishop of his times, died while swimming in the sea at Tramore on July 11, 1803.[12]

Cumberland was not actually recalled for several months, possibly because it was thought that his continued presence in Spain might counterfoil Jay's activities. The dramatist thought that at least one result of his sojourn in that country was the frustration of Jay's enterprises. But it should be remembered that after Cumberland's departure Jay found no more success in securing the recognition of the United States by Charles III. For reasons to be explained in the following chapter, Hillsborough on February 14, 1781, ordered Cumberland to return to England.[13]

11 AHN, *Est.* 4220, *Expdte.* 2, Docs. 143, 144, 145.
12 For brief summary of Thomas Hussey's life gathered from fugitive pieces of information, see *Dictionary of National Biography.*
13 Below, p. 117.

The entire English family Cumberland, now increased by one infant daughter born the previous August in Madrid, quit the Spanish capital on the 24th of March, 1781. Effusive farewells were said on both sides. Certainly Cumberland had received in Spain the greatest personal courtesy and consideration. If Spanish official folk had nothing but contempt for his lack of diplomatic parts and for his gullibility, they treated this enemy envoy with all the careful courtesy so natural to the immitigable Castilian. "You tell me that no more coud be done for me, was I an Ambassador," wrote Cumberland to Campo as he headed his mules and coach toward the French frontier. "I am persuaded of it, and never doubted but the Government of Spain would give as much to me thro' liberality as they concede to any Ambassador thro' Privelege. Let me say for the last time I shall speak of myself, that no Man ever enter'd Spain with a more conciliating disposition, and I hope I leave behind me some proofs of patience. Farewell!"[14]

If we are to believe Cumberland's *Memoirs*, Floridablanca took leave of him with even more lofty consideration than that reserved for foreign ambassadors. When Cumberland came out to the Pardo for a farewell audience, the Foreign Minister ended the interview with a final exquisite gesture in an inimitable Spanish way. He politely offered to reward Cumberland's peace efforts by paying to him the expenses which the envoy's own English Government had refused to remit. A playwright ought to have appreciated to the full a touch like this in such circumstances as those. Cumberland, as he refused the bounty, appears to have been moved by no sense of profound humiliation. Rather he

[14] Cumberland to Campo, March 20, 1781, AHN, *Est.* 4220, *Expdte.* 2, Doc. 193, also printed in Cumberland's *Memoirs*.

felt gratitude for the kindly feelings of the benevolent Floridablanca.

Not failing, on his part, in deep bows to the retreating enemy, Montmorin furnished passports for the return of Cumberland's family by way of France.

CHAPTER VII

THE touching farewell to Campo does not close our study of the Hussey-Cumberland affair. The principal interest of that mission to the student of the diplomatic history of the United States is its ominous relation to the question of American independence. We may see this in the reaction of French diplomacy to Florida-blanca's designs for a separate Gibraltar peace.

The precise value to the cause of American independence of Spanish intervention in the war has never been well calculated, nor will it be until some historian has studied adequately the naval history of all theatres of that great conflict. It is true that Spanish intervention gave the Bourbon allies a nominal naval superiority, and diverted portions of British forces to the West Indies and to Gibraltar. What had to be used there, of course, was of no service to England in North America. As we have seen, in 1779, the Franco-Spanish fleets controlled the Channel and threatened England itself with invasion. That the family allies were not able to take better advantage of this naval superiority is no measure of the lack of opportunity. It was a maritime preponderance which was much overvalued and consequently much sought after by the responsible leaders in both the United States and France, on the eve of Spain's declaration of war; indeed it is no exaggeration to say that they regarded it as almost essential to victory. But actually that intervention and the diversions that it caused seem to have been of no practical advantage to the United States nor to France, aside from the general moral effect of lining up another European power as an enemy of Great Britain. Whatever advantage might have been expected from occupying the energies of Great Britain in Europe was neutralized by the drawing away of French fleets and men to Gibraltar, Minorca, and the West Indies to satisfy Spain's requirements.

Nor was Spain of any real diplomatic assistance either to the United States or to France. So far as the United States was concerned she was a positive hindrance, for it soon became apparent that Spanish objectives in North America, the control of the Mississippi River and territorial conquests to the east of it, and to a lesser extent the conquest of the Floridas, were opposed to cherished and vital American interests. Furthermore Spain was plainly hostile to American independence. The Hussey-Cumberland negotiations reveal clearly enough her attitude on that point.

Spanish policy was also at odds with French diplomacy. These negotiations show how the Spanish alliance threatened to thwart the achievement of the great object of France's American alliance, which was the real reason for France's war against Great Britain—this same American independence. Vergennes soon found himself in a rather desperate position as middleman between two allies, both at war with Great Britain, but for widely different reasons: the United States for its own independence, which was also France's main object; Spain for Gibraltar and other objects which were not those of France at all. In his efforts, first to get Spain into the war, because of exaggerated hopes of the great assistance to be derived thereby in winning the war quickly; and secondly, once she had declared war, to keep her in and fighting, and prevent her from imposing a premature or even a separate peace, Vergennes was forced into successive concessions at the cost of his main objective. He was obliged to content himself with more and more imperfect definitions of what would constitute that American independence to which France stood pledged by the alliance of 1778. He first did this when he was obliged to run the danger of England's accepting the Spanish mediation offer of 1779 based on a truce *uti possidetis*. It was with this in mind that he had actually prepared the American Congress for a peace of independence by truce instead of treaty, but in the European negotiations which followed he was not then required to cross the *uti possidetis* bridge.[1]

This descent from a peace by definitive treaty to the idea of a peace by truce was the first qualification of the fullest concept of that liberty, sovereignty and indepen-

[1] After Great Britain's refusal of the Spanish mediation ultimatum and Spain's consequent declaration of war, Luzerne, French Minister in Philadelphia, delivered to Congress upon Vergennes's instructions the text of the Spanish ultimatum and other relevant papers as evidence of France's loyalty toward her American ally. The text of the Franco-Spanish convention of Aranjuez was of course not among these papers, nor does it ever appear to have been communicated to the United States. A delegate from Delaware to Congress whom La Luzerne describes as a man of distinguished talents said that although he had previously heard something of the Spanish terms he had found it difficult to believe them, so destructive was their nature to the American Union. "I begged him to consider the position and functions of a mediating power," relates La Luzerne, "and to tell me whether the impartiality which ought to characterize a mediator would permit the Catholic King to do more." The delegate was not unimpressed by this answer. "At the same time with some disquietude they asked me what would have been done in case the King of Great Britain had accepted the Spanish mediation. The only part, I replied, which could have been due to the King's glory and the engagements which he had contracted with you. His Majesty would have communicated to you the ultimatum, leaving you the choice of accepting or rejecting it, and in the latter case he would have continued the war jointly with you comformably to the treaties and principles of the alliance." La Luzerne to Vergennes, No. 27, Philadelphia, January 25, 1780. *Archives du Ministère des Affaires Etrangères, Correspondance Politique, Etats-Unis,* XI, fo. 88 (Library of Congress Transcripts).

dence absolute and unlimited, in matters of government as of commerce, which the Franco-American alliance called for; but it was a qualification allowed by the text of the treaty itself, which had stipulated for either explicit or tacit independence by treaty or by truce. After Spain was in the war Vergennes found himself vainly struggling against further concessions to Floridablanca at the cost of the main object of the American alliance. At first such concessions were on the border line and might be covered by plausible interpretations of the treaty of alliance. For example, the question of what was to be the territory of the United States whose independence was thus guaranteed. At first Vergennes had defined it as extending west to the Mississippi by the old charter grants of the colonies and including a natural right of navigation of that river to the sea. After Spain entered the war the claims of France's two allies clashed in the vast regions of that river, and Vergennes felt constrained to argue with his American allies that they should cooperate cordially with their new associate in the common war against Great Britain by settling the western boundaries with Spain by some reasonable compromise that would keep American territory at a respectable distance from the river. Though such arguments were never pushed aggressively they never completely subsided until the final peace. At this time (1779-1780) they were supported by a new interpretation of the treaty of alliance, namely that the guaranty of American independence did not apply to any specifically bounded territory, but to that region which was an intrinsic part of the thirteen States and which should be recognized as such by the eventual treaty of peace. This interpretation was another step away from the fullest conception of American independence; but in fairness to Vergennes it must be said that he did not attempt actually to force the United States to such a truncation of its western limits and that he abandoned the arguments (at least in America) as soon as he realized how opposed was Congress to such an arrangement.[2] Then came Hussey and Cumberland, whose advent in Spain was to prove that the *uti possidetis* danger had not passed when Great Britain rejected in 1779 the Spanish mediation ultimatum. Vergennes was now (1780 and 1781) to advance toward further concessions to Spain, concessions which in his own words were not allowable by the Franco-American alliance even by way of specious pretext. Here then is the importance of those negative negotiations of Cumberland and Hussey, which have been the subject of our previous chapters. The attitude to them of French diplomacy reveals how our one and only alliance, our very life-saving French alliance, involved the United States, unaware of the real scope of the danger, in the complications of purely European diplomacy, and how thus it threatened to defeat the object for which it was fashioned, signed and ratified. That this danger has hitherto not been fully realized does not make it any the less real nor does it diminish the historian's astonishment at the tremendous significance of the happy, the lucky victory of Yorktown.

We have seen that the Cumberland negotiations had been set on foot successfully by Hussey's first trip to Spain in January 1780, and that the envoy had been named before France knew anything about it, that only

2 For this phase of French policy see E. S. Corwin, *French Policy and the American Alliance,* Chap. x. For reappearance of this idea at the peace negotiations of 1782, see *ibid.,* XV; and S. F. Bemis, *Pinckney's Treaty,* 38-42.

after it was certain that Cumberland had been appointed and was to set out for Lisbon, that is to say, after it was sure that the mission would soon be known to the world, had Floridablanca thought it prudent to inform the French Court. From that moment on, the Hussey-Cumberland mission was a perfect nightmare for Vergennes. It had been that diplomatist's grand design to break up the British Empire by his American alliance, supported soon by a sequent Spanish alliance, then to assist in the erection of a formidable ring of armed neutral continental powers under whose protection naval supplies would be brought in to sustain and to increase the French fleet. Even now in 1780 his diplomacy with the neutral powers of Europe was coming to a head. If a separate peace should be made by Spain the whole great edifice for French victory would break down; French morale, strained as it was by increasing financial burdens of the war, would collapse; and France instead of retrieving her normal position in Europe might sink back below the level of the humiliation of 1763. Instead of the envisioned glorious triumph another dreadful defeat might follow Floridablanca's peace flirtations with England. It was to avoid such a catastrophe that Vergennes eventually felt compelled to consider a compromise on the basis of a Floridablanca formula.

Suspicions of separate Spanish conversations with England had been conveyed to Vergennes by the acute Montmorin shortly before Floridablanca's announcement of the expected visit of an English emissary. The French statesman's first reaction was one not of surprise but of real distrust and alarm. He saw through the whole Spanish stratagem at once. "In spite of the assurances which Monsieur le Comte de Floridablanca has given you that there is at present no question of any

negotiation," wrote Vergennes to Montmorin, "I confess that I am not without uneasiness; once one has
allowed oneself to go to the brink of infidelity, it is
always to be feared that one is likely to topple over."[3]
He realized that Spain had no interest in American
independence and to suit her own purposes would be
disposed to sacrifice France's engagements with the
United States. But he did not dare to demand that
France be admitted into these separate peace conversations; he knew that he could not insist, now that the
Spanish decision to listen to England's spokesman had
already been made. Nor was there any way to stop a
colloquy on Spanish soil. It therefore had to be understood that Floridablanca should listen to what the English had to say, and that if there were forthcoming any
serious offer it should be discussed between France and
Spain. With some considerable tautology Vergennes
and Louis XVI reiterated to Charles III and his foreign minister their professions of belief in the integrity
of the Spanish King and the dignity of his crown, particularly the sanctity of his engagements to his ally.
These were the professions that the circumstances
dictated.

"I do not deceive myself any more than you do,
Monsieur," wrote Vergennes to his ambassador,
April 21, 1780, "that if Spain treats separately it
is all up with American independence; but it would
be equally necessary to sacrifice that if we were ourselves to undertake any separate negotiation. That
is just the point of the dispute; the English have
not yet shown themselves disposed to yield this;
and they will stiffen to the extent that they perceive

3 No. 182 of April 21, 1780, Doniol, IV, 476.

less agreement and understanding between us and
Spain. If we cannot keep Spain from showing this
weak spot, let us take care that it is not seen in what
concerns us. It would be to dishonor ourselves gratuitously, drive the Americans to defection, and put
weapons in the hands of the English to prolong a
war which to my great astonishment Spain is even
more eager than ourselves to bring to a close. Remember, Monsieur, what I have imperatively told
you before, that if all this should end through an
injustice, the King risks less in suffering it than in
doing it. Damage to his interests could be repaired;
nothing would repay the loss of his reputation."[4]

It was further agreed that until the negotiations
should take some definite and serious turn they should
be kept secret from the Americans, though Vergennes
made it clear to Floridablanca that France could not
treat without the agreement of the United States, and
that it would be dangerous to delay beyond that point in
informing them. He suggested that in case of emer-
gency, John Adams, peace plenipotentiary of Congress
in Paris, or perhaps even Jay in Spain—in case his powers permitted—might be consulted.[5]

Before Floridablanca had even held his first conferences with Cumberland, Vergennes was beginning to
discover avenues of withdrawal out of the war and perhaps out of the American alliance, first by way of
Madrid, but soon rather by way of St. Petersburg.
Preparation for retreat is disclosed in his dispatches of
June 12, 1780, to Montmorin. In the first of these he
dwelt again on the English desire to create trouble be-

4 Doniol, IV, 453.
5 Vergennes to Floridablanca, April 26, 1780, AHN, *Est.* 4220, *Expdte.*
2, Doc. 54.

tween Spain and France over the question of American independence. He agreed with Montmorin's suggestions that it might be well to refresh the Spanish Minister's mind on the nature of France's engagements with the United States. For this it would be sufficient to show him again the text of the treaty of alliance of February 6, 1778. "The guaranty of the territories of the United States is eventual," he added suggestively; "its extent will not be fixed until the future pacification." In the second letter he stated to Montmorin that he felt there was some way of reaching an understanding if the English should be disposed to give up to the Americans the portions of their territory then occupied, that is those portions which were intrinsically a part of the thirteen states united, leaving them a *de facto* independence which they would enjoy by means of a long-time truce. "If I am not mistaken," noted Vergennes, "such was the first proposition of the King of Spain when he took upon himself the mediation [in 1779]; if that is what he would like to assure the Americans, the King would be able to employ his good offices to engage them to content themselves with it, and there would not be lacking good reasons to demonstrate to them that the means is not so important so long as they get the thing itself; but if it were a question of the second proposition which establishing the *uti possidetis* as the basis of a truce would cut off different parts of the United States, I see no reason, even a specious one, that could be given to induce them to be content with it, and if we think carefully of the King's essential interest, it is evident that it is not less opposed to this than are the Americans themselves."[6]

6 Doniol, IV, 459, 479-480.

A remark of Floridablanca to Montmorin that Spain would try to get for the American Colonies, in the approaching Cumberland negotiations, at least what they had been offered in the mediation ultimatum of 1779, aroused Vergennes's concern and at the same time indicated accurately enough the drift of Spanish policy: imperfect independence by long-time truce *uti possidetis*. Only weakly now did Vergennes argue against this, and most of his arguments were stockworn and long since perfectly ineffective with Floridablanca: a truce on the basis of the military *status quo* (said Vergennes) would leave the British and the Americans too near to each other, so close that they would be likely to make up with each other and jointly despoil Spain and France of their colonial dominions; Spain need not feel nervous on the other hand to see any independent American republican confederation arise on that continent, for it would be politically too impotent ever to have aggressive ambitions; moreover, in case of a long-time truce it would have to be guaranteed by Spain and France to be of any use—were it not better to escape being called upon to enforce such a guaranty by making independence effective once and for all?[7] We shall see that within eight months Vergennes was to be arguing that by virtue of the very proximity in which a long-time truce would leave British and Americans it might be an excellent thing, for it would leave them so close to each other as never to be good friends!

Vergennes was by now thoroughly convinced that at any time Spain might announce the terms of a peace settlement with Great Britain, including a truce *uti possidetis* for the American Colonies. The tenor of his

[7] See Vergennes to Montmorin, Nos. 119 and 120, of June 12, 1780, Doniol, IV, 459, 478.

dispatches shows that, protesting, he was being led by the diplomatic and military events of the war to reconcile himself to this pass and to attempt to line the Americans up to the terms of such an accommodation. He made a great effort to wean Spain away from supposed Gibraltar allurements of the British by sending Count d'Estaing to take charge at Cadiz of a joint expedition which Spanish assurances had led everybody at Versailles to suppose would be used to combine with de Guichen's fleet returning from the West Indies, the joint forces then rendezvousing at Brest for ulterior Channel operations. D'Estaing hurried to San Ildefonso, but found the Spanish Court unwilling to agree to any plans which would take their fleet toward England. After some weeks wasted in arguing, Spanish and French ships put to sea in late October from Cadiz with d'Estaing, but the Spanish contingent turned back to their home port as soon as the joint fleet passed Cape St. Vincent.[8]

D'Estaing's brief presence at San Ildefonso served to perturb Cumberland, who was also there at the time,[9] but accomplished little else. Meanwhile Floridablanca,

[8] Doniol, IV, 474.

[9] "I was at this time newly recovered from a mortification occasioned by a fractured arm and in the most reduced state imaginable, notwithstanding which no person dared to offer me the common salutations of civility, and wherever I presented myself in the Gardens of the Palace I created a solitude about me; even the bench was deserted on which I occasionally reposed myself. . . . The American Agent and his Secretary were caressed by the Court: I met d'Estaing in the gardens, with his head wounded by an overthrow of his coach and bandaged up. He was following the Suite of the Princess of Asturias who was walking the tour of the fountains according to her daily custom: he saluted me with good grace; our meeting attracted the eyes of the whole Court; he pleasantly observed to me that though our politics differed, our persons agreed in suffering the same mischance, both being maimed in the service. . . ." Cumberland's "Narrative of Secret Negotiations with Spain, 1780-1781," British Museum, *Additional MSS.*, 28851. (There is a transcript in the Library of Congress.)

heartened by the capture of the East and West India convoy in the summer and by the successes of Galvez in Florida, was urging on the French plans of his own which would have diverted more French ships and regiments to Gibraltar or the Caribbean. Vergennes and Montmorin were convinced that their Spanish ally was keeping Cumberland in Madrid partly as a means of coercing France into any Spanish military combination, on the ground that a refusal to follow in the lead of Spanish plans would be alleged as showing lack of proper cooperation and consequently exhibited as a reason for making separate peace with England.[10]

In North America the southern states of Georgia, North Carolina, and South Carolina were largely occupied by the British. According to La Luzerne the American armies were none too determined, and it seemed to be the British policy by studied considerate treatment of the inhabitants of the occupied "provinces" to attract them back to allegiance; in the South, he observed, the people appeared apathetic about independence and thoroughly tired of the war.[11]

The calendar of discouraging news was by no means yet complete, but before it was full Vergennes had turned to a new expedient, one originally recommended by the shrewd young Montmorin.[12] This was nothing less than bringing Russia in to redress the balance of power in western Europe which Vergennes believed to be threatened by the possibilities of a Spanish peace. Both Great Britain and France sedulously had courted

[10] Doniol, IV, 506.

[11] La Luzerne to Vergennes, July 17, and July 25, 1780, received September 12. *Archives du Ministère des Affaires Etrangères, Correspondance Politique, Etats-Unis*, XIII, 36. See also Vergennes's reply of October 22, 1780, *ibid.*, XIV, 155.

[12] Doniol, IV, 450.

Russian favor during the war.[13] The pronouncement of
the Armed Neutrality served notice to Europe that
French diplomacy had won the day at St. Petersburg.
In vain the British Government had tried to bribe
Catherine II with the island of Minorca to bring
about a peace without reference to American independence.[14] That woman was now at the apogee of her
prestige and eager to pose as the protector of Europe
by offering mediation to the belligerents. Peace through
Russian mediation would enhance the political reputation of the Empress. Peace would also put an end to the
tribulations of neutral powers and make it unnecessary
to call upon the armed neutrals for the performance of
positive acts.

Up to this point (August 1780) Vergennes had
fought shy of all mediators, Spanish, Austrian, or Russian. But pressure for peace was increasing. French
finances were rapidly weakening, and the Director
General, the famous Necker, in protest at the burdens
earnestly favored peace and did not scruple to let his
sentiments be known in England.[15] The Premier himself, the aged Maurepas, had already gone so far as to
write the mysterious letter which caused George III to
think that minister had some weighty reason for wishing
for peace.[16] Spain in an exultant mood and with Cum-

13 P. Fauchille, *La diplomatie française et la ligue des neutres de 1780*
(Paris, 1893); *Diaries and Correspondence of James Harris, Lord Malmesbury* (London, 1844).

14 *ibid.*, Malmesbury, I, 373; F. A. Golder, "Catherine II and the American Revolution," *Am. Hist. Rev.*, XXI, 92.

15 Doniol, IV, 492; *op. cit.*, II, 330.

16 See above, page 86; George III to Lord North, July 30, 1780, *Correspondence of King George the Third*, V, 103, 105. The text of this letter
which was written to N. P. Forth, a British secret-service agent who had
been in touch with Maurepas in 1778, is not revealed. December 1, 1780,
Necker wrote a secret letter to Lord North, suggesting a long-time truce
uti possidetis; but George III considered such a truce to be tantamount to

berland in reach at any moment was making exorbitant
naval demands on France for a campaign against
Jamaica. English newspapers of August 5, 1780, had
arrived in Paris with reports of an imminent peace with
Spain.[17] Louis XVI alarmed at the situation was urging
that his uncle Charles III actually be given a mandate
to make peace with England.[18] It was under these
ominous circumstances that Vergennes turned to
Russia.[19] Towards Spain he continued to maintain an
attitude of pretended trust; meanwhile he strove to
bring about a Russian mediation which would take the
peace lead out of Floridablanca's management. He
concluded that it were better to accept a compromise
peace at the hands of Catherine the Great as a mediator
than at the hands of Floridablanca as an ally. If necessary under adverse military circumstances he would
accept the idea of a truce *uti possidetis*—provided it
were presented *by a mediator*. If possible, he would
bring the Americans into line on that basis.

His mind made up, Vergennes refused to instruct
Montmorin to place the peace negotiations in Spanish
hands unless Louis XVI would give written instructions
and assume personal responsibility for such a fateful
act.[20] Such responsibility the King refused to take. The
Minister then rejected forthwith the Spanish importunities for a joint naval campaign for the capture of

independence for the Colonies. Lord Mahon, *History of England from the
Peace of Utrecht to the Peace of Versailles* (London, 1854), VII, Appendix, xiii; *Correspondence of King George the Third*, V, 163, 213. I have
not ascertained whether Vergennes was aware of this correspondence of
other individuals in the Cabinet.

17 Doniol, IV, 465, note 2.
18 September 1780, Doniol, IV, 487.
19 Vergennes to Montmorin, September 28, 1780, Doniol, IV, 487, 495.
20 *ibid.*, 488-493.

Jamaica.[21] Ostensibly frowning on the idea of a peace by long-term truce *uti possidetis,* strictly interpreted, he nevertheless went so far as to say to Montmorin (September 28, 1780) that France might accept such a peace if Great Britain would give up Long Island and New York, keeping perhaps Georgia and South Carolina. This could better be accepted, he stated, at the hands of Russia than from England through Spain, and he empowered Montmorin to suggest to Floridablanca the idea of a Russian mediation.[22]

The new orientation of French policy became more pronounced as the autumn and early winter months, 1780-1781, brought in a succession of unpromising if not desperate military advice and intelligence.

In Spain d'Estaing's cooperation with the Spanish fleet had broken down. On October 20 arrived from La Luzerne news of the American defeat at Camden and General Gates's rapid flight from the battlefield.[23] Shortly afterward there fell into Vergennes's possession that curious and suggestive interchange of letters between Lords Hillsborough and Stormont by which the former in vain offered to exchange places with the latter to enable him to propose and carry through a Spanish peace purchased with Gibraltar.[24] Toward the end of November came more news of the indifferent successes of the French expeditionary and naval forces in America. Letters from Ternay, *chef d'escadre* at Rhode Island, reported that the military situation was ex-

---

[21] *ibid.,* 496.

[22] Doniol, IV, 497. Verbal overtures to that effect had already been made to the Spanish *chargé* at St. Petersburg. Cumberland to Hillsborough, No. 4, Madrid, July 8, 1780, R.O., S.P.F., Series 94, Vol. 209.

[23] La Luzerne to Vergennes, September 2, 1780, received October 20. *Archives du Ministère des Affaires Etrangères, Correspondance Politique, Etats-Unis,* XIII, 167 (Library of Congress Transcript).

[24] Doniol, IV, 502. See above, page 94.

tremely uncertain, that the successes of the Revolution had been much overestimated in Europe.[25] At the same time Maria Theresa, Empress Mother of Austria, died,[26] and with her departed a moderating influence on the adventurous disposition of her son Joseph II, who it was feared might at any time upset the peace of the continent to the detriment of France, as indeed he had once done in 1778-1779 in the War of the Bavarian Succession. In December it was known that Guichen's fleet was returning without results from its long and costly cruise on the American station, with accounts of how the Spanish overseas squadron under Solano had refused to cooperate in an attack on St. Christopher's.[27] D'Estaing sailed in from Cadiz empty-handed, in January 1781. To top all this arrived in that month La Luzerne's dispatches up to December 21, full of reports of reverses in fact and in morale, and of demands of the United States for further support in men and in money.[28] On February 18 Franklin advised Vergennes that a special American plenipotentiary, John Laurens, was on his way to request from the French Government, following a conference between Washington and Rochambeau, 25,000,000 *livres* and another contingent of the French army. These generals believed this further assistance to be necessary if the war was to be won. With this information Franklin delivered a solemn appeal from Washington himself: "The actual situation makes essential either peace or the most vigorous efforts."[29]

Under these circumstances France began actively to seek, not merely to listen for peace. If in the autumn

25 Ternay to Vergennes, Rhode Island, September 10, 1780, *ibid.*, 434.
26 November 29, 1780.
27 Doniol, IV, 498.
28 *ibid.*, 539.
29 *ibid.*, 531.

of 1780 the English King had sent Hussey back to
Spain with a compromise offer, peace could have surely
been imposed on Floridablanca's terms. The French
Minister, already committed in his own mind to a truce
uti possidetis, would have been compelled to capitulate.
One can understand how Vergennes, amidst this ava-
lanche of evidence which seemed to demonstrate that the
American resistance was on the verge of collapse, con-
fronted with the imminent defection of Spain, his
government staggering under that enormous financial
burden which was eventually to bring the whole monarchy down in ruins, reached out hopefully for a Russian
mediation and reconciled himself with some alacrity to
that peace by truce *uti possidetis* at which at first his
gorge had risen. Such a policy, which was now definitely
crystallized in his mind, required a minimum of exchange of views and preparations with the Americans;
meanwhile the war must continue, and preparations
were to be made and resources stretched for one more
campaign, for the last chance of a final mighty blow, a
grand coup for victory. For this French and Spanish
naval policy were for once, though for opposite purposes, able to agree if not to combine. Guichen's fleet
was sent back under de Grasse with orders first to cooperate with the Spanish fleet to reinforce colonial stations in the West Indies. Following that, upon the
approach of winter, the Admiral was to sail north to
combine with French naval units from Newport and to
place himself at the disposal of Washington and Rochambeau for possible cooperation against the British
forces in some way to be worked out. This was the
happy inspiration of the whole war,—the still unseen
combination which was to snatch victory—and American independence—from defeat or fateful compro-

mise. Meanwhile, to content the Spanish, six French vessels proceeded from Brest to reinforce the Cadiz fleet confronting Gibraltar.[30] The French Ministry eventually furnished Laurens (May 16) with a subsidy of 6,000,000 *livres,* and France endorsed for the United States a loan of 10,000,000 *livres* to be raised in the Netherlands.[31] But when de Grasse left European waters for the Caribbean no one could foresee Yorktown. The Admiral had orders to take Rochambeau's troops off the continent and away to the West Indies, in case he should find the American army in process of dissolution.

The hoped-for mediation was rapidly developing. On December 12, 1780, Russia had made an oral mediation offer to France, and on the 16th of the same month to Great Britain in a formal written note. Vergennes accepted in principle but stated that he must first consult his allies.[32] Lord Stormont's reply was a request that Austria be invited to join them in the presentation of joint mediation offers. Meanwhile England declared war on Holland, December 19, 1780, thus jeopardizing the prestige of the Armed Neutrality (and making mediation a most agreeable function to Russia) and by belligerent treatment seeking to stop Dutch neutral carriage of naval stores to France. Under these provocative circumstances, England could not treat Catherine II's good offices too ungraciously. Actually Lord Stormont thought he saw a crowded opportunity to secure from Russia what England had been unable to get from Floridablanca: peace in Europe on the basis of the treaty of Paris of 1763, a peace which would leave Eng-

[30] Doniol, IV, 544-550.
[31] *ibid.*; Vergennes to Laurens, May 16, 1781, Wharton, IV, 418.
[32] Doniol, IV, 523.

land free to settle things directly and alone with the revolted colonies, a peace, in fine, which was to be bought by bribing the mediator. Under the utmost secrecy, Stormont, on January 20, 1781, addressed a dispatch to the British Ambassador at St. Petersburg, Sir James Harris, instructing him to offer to Catherine the Great the cession in full sovereignty of the island of Minorca (then beleaguered by Spanish attacking forces), if the Empress would successfully use her influence as a mediator to bring about a peace on this basis, accompanied by a total withdrawal of French forces from North America, with no stipulation whatsoever concerning the Colonies. Simultaneously with the signature of such a treaty, George III would sign over Minorca to the Czarina.[33] On February 14 Hillsborough directed Cumberland to return straightway from Madrid,[34] presumably because no mediation could make headway as long as direct conversations were continuing between England and Spain.

Russia straightway invited Austria's joint offices (January 10),[35] thus satisfying the English request in that particular, but Catherine II judiciously refused the Minorca bait. It was Prince Kaunitz, the conceited veteran Austrian Minister of Foreign Affairs, seeking retaliation for the successful and embarrassing Franco-Russian mediation at Teschen in 1779 between Prussia and Austria, and eagerly desiring to preside over a peace congress at Vienna, who finally drafted the definite mediation proposals, May 1781, which were handed to Vergennes jointly by the Austrian and Rus-

[33] *Diaries and Correspondence of Lord Malmesbury*, I, 373.
[34] R.O., S.P.F., Series 94, Vol. 209.
[35] Doniol, IV, 513.

sian diplomatic representatives at Versailles.[36] These were in the shape of articles designed to induce the belligerents to agree to send peace plenipotentiaries to Vienna, articles which Kaunitz said were formulated on the principle that one power ought not to lay down conditions of peace which it could not accept were it in the other's place. Kaunitz proposed, in the name of the mediating powers: (1) that all belligerents meet at Vienna, but that Great Britain and the "American Colonies" treat separately for American peace, without the intervention of the other belligerents, nor even of the imperial mediating courts unless such mediation were requested and granted; (2) that the separate Anglo-American peace be signed only conjointly and simultaneously with the other (European) peace settlement, neither peace settlement to have effect without the other, and both to be guaranteed by the mediating powers and such other neutrals as the belligerents might invoke for that purpose; (3) an armistice for one year pending negotiations. These articles appeared to afford Great Britain a pretext for accepting on the ground that no power stood between her and her revolted colonies in the proposed parley.

When he received the Austro-Russian proposal Vergennes already had carefully formulated his peace policy and put it down in a confidential memorandum. It was a policy which, allowing for some diplomatic bargaining, was conducive to a compromise peace by mediation on the basis of *uti possidetis*. Meanwhile the French navy and expeditionary forces were making the final effort in the campaign of 1781. If these last mili-

---

[36] D'Arneth et Flammermont, *Correspondance secrète du Comte de Mercy-Argenteau avec l'Empereur Joseph II et le Prince de Kaunitz* (Paris, 1889), I, 37, note 1.

tary efforts should fail or be interrupted by disaster, Vergennes was ready to go ahead rapidly toward peace without victory. If a crowning military stroke—another Saratoga—should come out of America before the end of the year, these plans for retreat need never see the light of day. The February 1781 memorandum in which he dictated to his secretary Rayneval his peace plan has never received sufficient attention. It is cited by Bancroft and it is printed in part by Henri Doniol. But the eminent French historian has only incidentally referred to this important document, and, in a footnote, by some inadvertence has printed only the final recapitulating paragraphs, which by no means bring out its full significance.[37] In the appendix to this volume we are printing for the first time the complete text of the document. A perusal of the entire document, of which the skilfully worded recapitulating paragraphs are presented in translation in the footnote to this page,[38] will

[37] Doniol, IV, 553, note 1.

[38] "Summing up the previously considered details, one notes the following propositions:

"(1) It is up to the author of the war, the King of England, to make sacrifices to obtain peace.

"(2) The first of these sacrifices to make is the independence of North America.

"(3) This independence may be assured either by a definitive treaty or by a truce.

"(4) Whatever be the form adopted, the King of England may, with the intervention of the two mediating powers, treat directly with the Americans.

"(5) The truce will be a long-time one, for 20, 25, 30 years, etc. The United States will be treated as independent in fact, and no restriction will be placed upon the exercise of their sovereign rights.

"(6) It is to be desired that the *status quo* might be avoided, but in case this is not possible, it should be limited to South Carolina and Georgia, and the evacuation of New York should be stipulated.

"(7) The King cannot make any proposition for truce to Congress if it is coupled with the *status quo*, but by separating these two propositions His Majesty can engage to bring Congress to subscribe to the truce, if he has a secret assurance that New York will be excepted.

"(8) In case of a truce, the King will propose to the Americans, if there

show that Vergennes was now proposing a peace by a 20- to 30-year truce *uti possidetis,* except for New York, which must be evacuated by the British, with independence *de facto* for the United States. Paragraph 7 says that the King can make no proposition for truce to Congress if it is coupled with the principle of the military *status quo,* "but by separating these two conditions His Majesty will be able to induce Congress to subscribe to the truce, if he has a *secret*[39] assurance that New York will be excepted." The *body* of the memoir explains that a proposal of a truce *uti possidetis* to the United States would be in "some sense" a violation of the treaty of alliance which guaranteed the independence of every one of the thirteen States; but that though France therefore could not propose this to Congress, the mediators, who were not bound in any way, might propose it, *after* the American plenipotentiaries had been brought to the peace conference—further, it would not be well to announce such an idea beforehand!

That very minister who eight months previously had argued that a truce *uti possidetis* would leave the British

be need for it, a new convention the object of which will be to assure them against English attacks upon the expiration of the truce.

"It may be well to finish the present memoir by the following remark. The King has made war on Great Britain not by choice but by necessity. Until now His Majesty has made the greatest exertions to sustain the burden of it; should he be willing to lose the fruits of so much expense by yielding the principal object at issue? Such a sacrifice could not be justified except after the greatest reverses impossible to repair. Were it the fruits of weakness or inconstancy it would tarnish forever His Majesty's glory and reputation. The resources of England are on the point of exhaustion; she is without an ally, and her forces are inferior to those of the House of Bourbon; in such a state of affairs the King's magnanimity may be invoked; but his condescension must not impugn either his dignity or his interest."

For full text of memoir, see Appendix No. 12.

[39] Italics inserted. The term *status quo* is used here to indicate *uti possidetis.*

and Americans so close to each other that they might reach a reconciliation and fall on French and Spanish colonial possessions in the new world, argued that such a truce, New York excepted, would be a good thing because the British and the Americans, so close to each other, would be continually distrustful and quarrelling; this salutary condition of affairs would prevent any political or commercial understanding between them, and the Americans, seeking the continued friendship and protection of the King of France, would also gradually transfer their foreign commerce to that monarchy. Vergennes, it must be said, was never at loss for an argument to support any step he might find it necessary to consider.

French peace policy thus fixed, it remained to line up the Americans so that they could be led unsuspecting to a peace conference without previous restrictions to endanger the success of such a conference on the lines now formulated by Vergennes. Toward this end Vergennes's instructions to La Luzerne had been gradually working. In 1779 when the Spanish mediation appeared imminent Vergennes had instructed La Luzerne's predecessor, Conrad Alexandre Gérard, to warn Congress of such a negotiation and to bring about the appointment of an American plenipotentiary who might be in Europe for the purpose of representing the United States. Gérard had been instructed to draw up a new treaty with the United States by which in case of a truce at that time France would guarantee independence.[40]

After a protracted debate over peace terms, Congress appointed John Adams as a plenipotentiary. He ar-

[40] Doniol, IV, 529. Vergennes to La Luzerne, No. 3, October 1, 1779, *Archives du Ministère des Affaires Etrangères, Correspondance Politique, Etats-Unis*, X, 55 (Library of Congress Transcript).

rived in Europe long after the outbreak of war between England and Spain. Failure of the Spanish mediation by then had rendered unnecessary any further Franco-American treaty negotiations, and La Luzerne, acting on instructions, dropped that idea. When Adams reached France early in 1780, he did not consider that new circumstances had suspended his functions. His instructions empowered him to make a treaty of peace and independence and another treaty of commerce with England, without reference to particular circumstances, and he argued at great length and somewhat testily to Vergennes that it might be desirable straightway to communicate to Great Britain his nomination for that purpose. Vergennes felt that the gratuitous revelation of a readiness to make peace—no matter how stiff its terms might be—would encourage the Anglo-Spanish peace negotiations then under way. With difficulty he persuaded Adams to refrain from this contemplated step. Vergennes suspended correspondence with Adams as an impossible peacemaker, and limited his intercourse for the time being to the regular minister, Franklin.[41] The unmanageable Adams went off to the Netherlands to seek diplomatic support that might be more independent of French control. Vergennes instructed La Luzerne to suggest to Congress that Adams was not the appropriate person to be entrusted with the negotiations of peace.[42] The imminence and complications of compromise peace negotiations made it desirable that conduct of the whole business be as much as possible under France's control. Vergennes on March 9, 1781,

[41] For the correspondence, see Wharton, III, 300, 492, 496, 509, 518, 564, 580, 664-7, 670, 699, 809, 827-8, 848, 861, 870, 872; IV, 3-14, 16, 18.

[42] To La Luzerne, No. 8, August 7, 1780, *Archives du Ministère des Affaires Etrangères, Correspondance Politique, Etats-Unis,* XIII, 101.

therefore instructed La Luzerne to cause Congress to
put Adams under the direction of the French Foreign
Minister and to induce the American Government to
revise the plenipotentiary's instructions in view of the
immediate possibilities of peace, either through Cumberland's maneuvers—that emissary was still in Spain—
or, more likely, through the Austro-Russian mediation
now expected. Congress would do well to imitate the
example of the King and declare in principle that it
would be disposed to receive peace from the hands of
the mediators; it could rely on the justice of the two
sovereigns who had tendered their good offices; and it
could trust to the defense of its interests by the King of
France. As to actual American peace terms, remarked
Vergennes, coming to the important point, it would be
more or less premature to discuss them, for such a discussion would give place to endless deliberations that
would turn Congress aside from the main object, which
was the establishment of the mediation. "You will remark moreover to the principal members of Congress
that it is possible that the difficulty of effecting a definitive peace may lead the mediators to propose a truce,
and that it is consequently necessary for the plenipotentiary of the United States to be eventually authorized
to make known their determination on this object." In
explaining these new circumstances Vergennes observed
to La Luzerne that the English would doubtless not be
moderate in renouncing all that vast western territory
claimed by the United States; but Congress must feel
the necessity of capturing the goodwill of the mediators
by itself exercising every possible moderation and reserve—except for independence, which, asserted Vergennes, was not possible of modification.[43] France had

[43] Vergennes to La Luzerne, No. 14, March 9, 1781, *Archives du Ministère*

long since ceased actively to support the western claims of the United States, and since the ideas of compromise had gained headway in Vergennes's mind he had introduced into his dispatches a tone of suggestion for La Luzerne to follow, that if Congress itself was not able to sustain the wavering allegiance of the population of the occupied southern states certainly France was not obliged to go any further to include those regions within the treaty guaranty.[44] By the content of the memorandum of February 1781 we have seen that Vergennes would be willing, in case the 1781 campaign were fruitless, to accept—always ostensibly at the hands of mediators—a truce *uti possidetis* except for the restitution of the strategic town of New York. These instructions to La Luzerne of the following March 9, closed with this significant paragraph: "You will advise the President of Congress that in case the mediation offer of the two imperial courts should take such a turn that His Majesty be obliged to give a categoric answer, His Majesty will accept conditionally for himself and the United States. This step will not be too inconvenient since nothing now hinders them from following the example of the King and placing their interests in the hands of such just and enlightened mediators, and a refusal to do so would bring on disastrous and incalculable results."

The proposed preliminary articles of the mediating powers, of May 27, 1781, were not of such a character, nor was the unchanged military situation so hopeless as to require Vergennes thus arbitrarily to accept mediation in the name of the United States. Moreover, by that

des Affaires Etrangères, Correspondance Politique, Etats-Unis, XV, 90 (Library of Congress Transcripts).

[44] Vergennes to La Luzerne, Versailles, October 22, 1780, No. 9., *ibid.,* XIV, 151.

time Cumberland had left Spain, and with his departure vanished the immediate menace of a Spanish peace. But the receipt of the preliminary articles made it necessary at least to discuss them with the only American plenipotentiary then available and authorized to treat of peace, namely the objectionable John Adams, who was summoned from The Hague for that purpose. Adams was willing enough to proceed to Vienna or anywhere else to discuss peace terms, and to discuss them separately with Great Britain; but he insisted on going there as the acknowledged representative of the sovereign and independent United States of America.[45] He immediately saw through the *status quo* stratagem and argued against it to Vergennes with the utmost vigor. In this acuteness and this determination he evinced an attitude which was resolutely exhibited by John Jay and himself in a critical period of the final peace negotiations of 1782.

A glance at our map of parts of the United States held by British and by Spanish forces in June 1781, will show what Great Britain—and Spain, let it not be forgotten—might have claimed on the principle of *uti possidetis*. Observe the significance of such claims not only in New York City, Long Island, Wilmington, Charleston, and Savannah, but along the northern frontier, particularly in the Great Lakes region and the far northwest; and in the southwest, where the Spanish had captured

---

[45] "I may say further, that as there is no judge upon earth of a sovereign power but the nation that composes it, I can never agree to the mediation of any powers, however respectable, until they have acknowledged our sovereignty, so far at least as to admit a minister plenipotentiary from the United States as the representative of a free and independent power. After this we might discuss questions of peace or truce with Great Britain without her acknowledging our sovereignty, but not before." John Adams to the President of Congress, Paris, July 11, 1781, Wharton, IV, 560. For Adams's correspondence with Vergennes in regard to the mediation proposals, the *status quo,* etc., see Wharton, IV, 571, 576, 589.

West Florida, and had sent detachments across the river from Fort St. Louis and Fort Arkansas to claim territory on the east bank, north and south of the Ohio.

Fortunately for the United States the unequivocal reply (June 15, 1781) of George III's Government to the proposed preliminary articles of May 1781, refusing to participate in any mediation conference at which the American plenipotentiaries should even be present,[46] relieved France (and Spain,[47] who had refused to consider mediation at all so long as Cumberland had remained at her Court, that is to say, to March 1781) from any immediate necessity of committing herself in any way to the Austro-Russian offer, and gave a chance to await the issue of the campaign overseas. It further eased Vergennes from what would have been a most uncomfortable encounter with the perspicacious if truculent Adams. The reply of Vergennes to the mediators, in August 1781, was nevertheless in thorough conformity to the program laid down in his February memoir.[48]

[46] Flassan, *Histoire de la diplomatie française*, VII, 317. For text of reply, see Wharton, IV, 445.

[47] Dánvila y Collado, *Reinado de Carlos III*, V, 340-352.

[48] D'Arneth et Flammermont, *Correspondance secrète de Mercy-Argenteau avec l'Empereur Joseph II et le Prince de Kaunitz*, I, 60, 66, note 1, fixes the date for this reply, which is mistakenly dated in the English translation sent home by Adams and printed in Wharton, IV, 441-444, and 860-863. Apparently the date printed in Wharton is the date of the first delivery of the Austro-Russian proposals to Vergennes, not of his reply to them.

Vergennes replied: (1) that he stood by Spain in her demands for Gibraltar as a part of the definitive peace treaty, not as a sequent separate treaty; (2) that the King of France would be willing to invite "the Americans" to the peace conference, for a separate negotiation with Great Britain—the same to go hand in hand with that of the Courts of Madrid and Versailles—provided he could do so in such a way as not to render France suspect by causing them to fear for their political existence; (3) any truce must be a long-time truce, not a simple one-year armistice; (4) as to the proposed *status quo*, "neither France nor Spain has any reason to reject it, so far as they are individually concerned. This is not

On receipt of unsatisfactory answers from both sides, Kaunitz decided to postpone the mediation proposals to more propitious and more decisive circumstances.[49]

It was the British answer which had made the mediation impossible. France had been amenable to a "middle term" in regard to American independence, at the hands of the mediators, and Vergennes had made use of Floridablanca's own phrase in suggesting it to Austria and Russia;[50] but George III would not listen to compromise. After this, peace for France, and for the United States, must be a peace of victory or a peace of defeat. A margin of only seven days brought the victory of Yorktown.[51] The treaty of 1782 was therefore a peace of absolute and unlimited, let us say of implacable independence. Mediators had nothing to do with it, except in a nominal and honorific capacity at the signature of the final articles in 1783.

The colorful Hussey-Cumberland negotiations of 1779-1781 portended great events which did not come to pass. Their very negative character has hitherto lost them the fullest scrutiny of historians. Despite their unsuccess they have been worthy of our study. They mapped out a possible page of history of the utmost instruction to the student of the foundation of American foreign policy. With hurricane warnings set and a rocky

the case with the Americans. To be satisfied of this, we need only cast our eyes upon the *points* that the British troops actually occupy upon the continent of North America. The question will then be to obtain the consent of the United States, *and this consent can only be demanded by the two courts that offer their mediation* [italics inserted], for the reasons that have already been urged."

[49] Wharton, IV, 446, for text of reply of the two mediating courts. See also Joseph II to Mercy-Argenteau, October 27, 1781, d'Arneth et Flammermont, *op. cit.*, I, 69.

[50] Flassan, *op. cit.*, 308.

[51] The British relieving fleet arrived off the Virginia capes seven days after the surrender of Cornwallis.

shore on his lee, Vergennes had reefed his canvas and
chartered a track through supposedly tumultuous seas
toward the port of compromise. Rather unexpectedly he
was able to guide his many-masted diplomatic craft under full sail beneath serene skies into the haven of complete victory. The highly interesting and still imperfectly understood history of the peace negotiations of
1782 is beyond the scope of this essay; but one who has
followed the vicissitudes of the Franco-American alliance to the eve of those final negotiations can only ad-
mire the resolute hearts and firm touch with which the
able American peace commission with sure instinct finally brought their little ship through waters still not wholly charted for them. For Congress had readily and trust-
ingly yielded to the importunities of Vergennes and
accepted the mediation. Four other negotiators, Laurens, Jay, Jefferson, and Franklin, were added to the
commission, sharing with Adams the powers formerly
lodged exclusively with that son of Massachusetts. In
revamped instructions for the commission, formulated
under the guidance of the skilful La Luzerne, there were
only two indispensable conditions precedent: independence according to the "form and effect" of the treaties
of February 6, 1778, with France, and the unimpaired
maintenance of those treaties. Congress innocently and
gratefully placed its plenipotentiaries under the advice
and direction of the King of France, through his ministers, on all problems of the peace negotiations, in order
that they might make peace "as circumstances may direct, *and as the state of the belligerents and the disposition of the mediating powers may require.*" The last
paragraph of the instructions stated that the plenipotentiaries were at liberty to accept a truce, "or to
make such other concessions as may not affect the sub-

stance of what we contend for, and providing that Great Britain be not left in possession of any part of the United States."

At Vienna under the circumstances envisaged by Vergennes, in the spring of 1781, the state of the belligerents certainly would have dictated peace by truce; the disposition of the mediating powers, secretly supported by France, would have required the terms *uti possidetis*. Under these circumstances would the American Commission have withstood the pressure put on them to leave Great Britain in possession of the parts of the United States then held by British troops? We cannot tell. Yorktown put an entirely different aspect on the negotiations which took place at Paris the following year. In those negotiations the American commissioners very properly broke their instructions to take every step in the full confidence and under the advice and direction of the ministers of the French King. The experience of Adams and Jay in Madrid and Paris, during the years when the dramatist Cumberland was led by the priest Hussey to his one performance on the great stage of European politics, was not amiss when these two younger American envoys came to the assistance of the urbane and supple Franklin in the very positive negotiations which ended in a real independence.[52]

[52] In the light of the above chapters, it is pertinent to quote the entire instructions of Congress, of June 15, 1781, to the peace commission, Messrs. Adams, Franklin, Jay, Laurens and Jefferson: "You are hereby authorized and instructed to concur, in behalf of these United States, with his most Christian majesty in accepting the mediation proposed by the Empress of Russia and the Emperor of Germany.

"You are to accede to no treaty of peace which shall not be such as may, 1st, effectually secure the independence and sovereignty of the thirteen United States, according to the form and effect of the treaties subsisting between the said United States and his most Christian majesty; and 2dly,

The Cumberland family reached London in the summer of 1781, after the playwright diplomatist, destitute of funds, had nearly died of fever at Bayonne. Only a loan from a kind-hearted fellow traveller enabled him to get his dependents safely home. During his stay in Spain his expenses had risen far above his official emoluments. There appears to have been no precise financial agreement between him and the government which had employed him on that mission. Cumberland understood that Mr. Secretary Robinson would honor all the drafts on his London bankers which he should draw while abroad. But Mr. Secretary Robinson did no such thing. Cumberland got only one thousand pounds, which was advanced to him when he set out for Lisbon. During the time in which his family travelled and lived on the peninsula like Spanish grandees or English nobility, he exhausted his own fortune and what was left of his

in which the said treaties shall not be left in their full force and validity.

"As to disputed boundaries and other particulars, we refer you to the instructions given to Mr. John Adams, dated 14th of August, 1779, and 18th of October, 1780, from which you will easily perceive the desires and expectations of Congress. But we think it unsafe, at this distance, to tie you up by absolute and peremptory directions upon any other subject than the two essential articles above mentioned. You are, therefore, at liberty to secure the interest of the United States in such a manner as circumstances may direct, and as the state of the belligerents and the disposition of the mediating powers may require. For this purpose you are to make the most candid and confidential communications upon all subjects to the ministers of our most generous ally, the King of France; to undertake nothing in the negotiations for peace or truce without their knowledge and concurrence; and ultimately to govern yourselves by their advice and opinion, endeavoring in your whole conduct to make them sensible how much we rely upon his majesty's influence for effectual aid in everything that may be necessary to the peace, security, and future prosperity of the United States of America.

"If a difficulty should arise in the course of the negotiations for peace from the backwardness of Great Britain to acknowledge our independence, you are at liberty to agree to a truce, or make such other concessions as may not affect the substance we contend for, and provided that Great Britain be not left in possession of any part of the United States." Wharton, IV, 504.

wife's. A government entirely unimpressed by his value as a diplomatist ungenerously refused to reimburse him. He wrote unanswered appeals, before and after his return to England, to the King's notorious disbursing agent. There was even more woe in store for him. When the North Government fell, including Cumberland's protectors, the Opposition was able to carry the bill for the abolition of the Board of Trade and Plantations. Anxious Cumberland applied to Shelburne, the new secretary of state for the southern department, in whose office (which included home and what was left of colonial affairs) it was suggested that the Board's records might be incorporated. Flattering himself that he could be useful, he prayerfully and respectfully offered his services to assist Shelburne and his colleagues in power that they might "effect the rescue of this sinking Empire."[53]

The Empire did not sink, if Cumberland's fortunes did. In vain he composed for Shelburne a lengthy memorandum on his Spanish mission, trying to emphasize the value of his services, and soliciting a recompense. Cumberland fell back on one half his former stipend, and the uncertain emoluments of his literary endeavors. Shortly after his return to London he presented a new play, *The Walloons,* in which an Irish priest, Padre O'Sullivan, appears in the character of a spy. Reading this new comedy on the continent, the indignant Hussey discerned that O'Sullivan was modelled on himself.[54] Fancy Hussey imagining such a thing! But relations between the priest and playwright continued on an

[53] Cumberland to Shelburne, Portland Place, Friday morning, March 29, 1782. I am indebted to Dr. R. G. Adams of the W. L. Clements Library for securing for me a transcript of this letter remaining in the Lansdowne Papers at Bowood.

[54] Hussey to Campo, Bologna, June 22, 1782, AHN, *Est.* 4220, *Expdte.* 2, Doc. 147.

ostensibly friendly basis, if we are to believe Hussey's communications to Campo from various parts of Europe.

After years of voluminous writing, Cumberland in 1807 published his celebrated, heavy, pedantic, and, to the twentieth century reader, most tedious *Memoirs,* for which he got £500 from the publisher, which money he mentions when revealing certain never-before-printed letters addressed, after his return from Spain, to Mr. Secretary Robinson. These memoirs, in no way damaging to Cumberland, his ravishing daughters and really heroic wife, but confessedly unreliable as to details and dates, and incomplete as to the inner history of the Spanish adventure; together with the narrative and argumentative manuscript *Memorial*[55] now in the British Museum, have until now served as the imperfectly reliable sources for what little has been written in English of his famous trial in the field of diplomacy.[56]

Such was the history of the Hussey-Cumberland mission. A failure in the attempt to bring about secret peace arrangements between Great Britain and Spain, it did not fail because of the impossibility, under any and all circumstances, of splitting Spain away from the Family Compact. It collapsed because of the obstinacy of the British King. George III at that time was unwilling to pay the high price of Gibraltar. With equally decisive stubbornness, he resisted every attempt to carry the subject of the American Colonies into peace negotiations between himself and his traditional European enemies. This fine obstinacy saved the cause of perfect American independence.

[55] *Additional MSS.* 28851, "Narrative of Secret Negotiations with Spain, 1780-1781" (Library of Congress Transcript).

[56] The accounts in French (Doniol) and in Spanish (Urtazun, and Dánvila) rest either on limited sources or on inadequate exploitation of them.

APPENDIX

NO. 1

FLORIDABLANCA'S FIRST UNSIGNED MEMORANDUM FOR HUSSEY,
JANUARY 1780[1]

Lo que he podido explorar, y descubrir tratando con el Ministerio, con pretexto de habilitar una pension Ecc^{ca}. que me fue concedida dos años há, se reduce a que S M Cat^{ca}: está resuelto à seguir la Guerra con el mayor teson, y à que tenga efecto una fuerte invasion en Inglaterra, a lo que parece averse obligado la Francia: que sin embargo, siendo el Rey Catholico de un caracter Religioso y pio puede esperarse que para evitar la efusion de sangre humana se le moverìa a tratar de paz siempre que la Inglaterra se preste à algun acomodemiento util a la España en el qual se salve el honor de S M C y su palabra empeñada ya con la Francia por el discuido y extravagante conducta que en los dos años pasados tuvo el antecedt^{te}: Ministerio: Que este punto de salvar el honor y empeños contrahidos por S M Cat^{ca}: es el mas difficil, mediante la natural bondad y probidad de este Monarca, cuia palabra mira como el Vinculo mas sagrado de la tierra: Que por Fortuna hasta aora no se ha empeñado el Rey Cat^{ca} con las Colonias pero se espera de un dia a otro al S^r. Jai Presidente que fue del Congreso, y encargado de tratar de este asunto, y corre priesa atajar esta negociacion: pues Si el Rei de España hace algun tratado con las Colonias seria imposible reducirle à que falte à el y los negocios serán irremediables: Que el Rei Cath^{co}: jamas cederá la pretension de Gibraltar en que toda la nacion se halla tan inflamada, que hasta los Clerigos Frailes, y Monjas han ofrecido quanto tienen para esta Guerra y que si huviera un medio de evacuar ésta plaza con el pretexto de faltar los viveres, y ser necessario preservar la Guarnicion, para

---

[1] Original in AHN, *Est.* 4220, *Expdte.* 2, Doc. 71. There are three copies of this document: a first draft, in Floridablanca's hand, unsigned; a fair copy; and a third copy in Hussey's hand, unsigned. The Hussey copy, the one taken to England, is reproduced here. In reproducing the texts of the several pieces in this Appendix, I have preserved the original imperfect spelling, accents, and punctuation.

emplearla, ô en defenza de la misma Inglaterra, ô en la Guerra mas util de las Islas de America ô Colonias podria exigirse y esperarse una Capitulacion honrosa en que la Inglaterra obtuviese la paga de la artilleria, y efectos militares y ademas la palabra del Rei de España de no ligarse con las Colonias, ô de no insistir en la invasion de la Inglaterra: ô de ambas cosas. pero si esto no que quedaba efectuado antes de Concluir Febrero llegarìa tarde qualquier ajuste por la venida del Ministro de las Colonias, y por las medidas tomadas para abrir la Campaña y S M C no se fiará de palabras Sobre Gibraltar por el Engaño que dice se hizo à su Padre en tiempo de Jorge 1º.

Tambien me parece que si la Inglaterra asegurase no invadir las posessiones Españolas de America y Islas Philipinas se podria obtener del Rey Cath^{co} que no invadiese las possesiones Inglesas ô suspendiese la continuacion de las invadidas con tal que en la Florida se tomase algun temperamento y que se hiciese algun arreglo por lo tocante a Honduras y Campeche.

Si todo esto se evacuase pronto restableciendo la Confianza del Rei de España; aunque éste nunca faltaria à sus empeños con la Francia, se le podria mover à que indugese, como tanbien à las Colonias, a algunos medios de ajuste, y à algun género de dependencia de las mismas Colonias, respecto de su Metropoli; à cuio fin se podrian conceder algunos puntos.

Pero si la negociacion que propongo se introduce entodo, ô en parte, será preciso guardar el mayor secreto y fidelidad; pues qualquier abuso que hiciese la Inglaterra, acabarra de hecharlo a perder todo para siempre—

NO. 2

FLORIDABLANCA'S SECOND UNSIGNED MEMORANDUM FOR HUSSEY,
JANUARY 1780[1]

Hussey RESERVADO

Nota de los Especies que he averiguado, y de otras que me occurren *para mi govierno*.

El Comodore Johnstone se valiò en Lisboa de Dⁿ. Luis Cantofer, paraque propusiese, como efectivamente propuso, al Ministerio Español, que si abrasava la neutralidad, cederian los Ingleses à Gibraltar, pagandoles los efectos militares que alli tienen à justa tasacion, y que si la España auxiliase para Sujetar las Colonias, se le cederia la Florida, y admiteria à la pesca de la terra nova

Johnstone tuvo la imprudencia de hablar en la mesa, de la cesion de Gibraltar, delante de muchas personas, y de dos oficiales Españoles; y El Ministerio de España, creyendo que toda esta publicidad es una maniovra para indisponerla con la Francia, avisó à esta del paso dado por Johnstone; y respondió à Cantofer rehusando entrar en materia sobre este asunto.

Si se intenta é insiste en que la España embie persona à Inglaterra que trate los asuntos, se confirmará en que la idea es desunirla y embaracarla con la Francia, luego que se sospeche ô descubra, como es natural, que se trata algo: y asi sera, à mi parecer, tiempo perdido, usar de este medio.

Si se gana la Confianza del Rei de España, por la evacuacion de Gibraltar; y se obtiene, que no se ligue con las Colonias, ni se empeñe en una invasion de Inglaterra, con lo demas que separadamente propondre, se lograba desde luego una specie de neutralidad mui util, y se podria poner à S M C en que promoviese nuestros intereses con la Francia para una pacificacion en que no entrase el punto de la Independencia.

Este será el Escollo de qualquiera tratado porque ligada la Francia con las Colonias no querrà ceder si no son reconnocidas;

1 Original in AHN, *Est.* 4220, *Expdte.* 2, Doc. 74. There are two copies: a first draft in Floridablanca's hand, unsigned; and another copy in Hussey's hand, unsigned. The Hussey copy, taken to England, is reproduced here.

y para esto podria tomarse el temperamento de reconnocer ellas una dependiencia feudal, (vaga) como las Ciudades libres del Imperio: ampliando ô restringiendo los derechos del Soberano segun la proporcion que huviese.

Por éste ô otro medio que pareciese al Rei de Inglaterra podria trabajar la Españ⸗ con la Francia, y aun con Monsr Jai, si quiere el Ministerio Brit^{co}: pero seria menester pensar en los partidos que se harian à la Francia para irla desprendiendo de los empeños de Independiencia absoluta que ha tomado por las Colonias; y suavisará éstas el Yugo que temen en la Sugecion.

En quanto à la España: ésta querria ademas de Gibraltar, poner regla en los establecimientos, de Campeche, y Honduras; y adquerir la porcion de la Florida que esta de la parte de adentro del Canal de Bahama, en que se incluie Pensacola, y la Mobila, aunque lo demas quedase à la Inglaterra, con la Ciud^d: de San Augustin, y sus pertenencias. Repito que en mi dictamen todo dependeria, de poder ganar la Confianza del Rey de España, con la evacuacion generosa y pronta de Gibraltar en cambio de impedir su alianza, con las Colonias, y una invasion de Inglaterra

INDIVIDUAL OPINIONS OF MEMBERS OF THE SPANISH COUNCIL OF
MINISTERS ON THE QUESTION OF SEPARATE PEACE NEGOTIATION
WITH GREAT BRITAIN, FEBRUARY 29, 1780[1]

OPINION OF DON MIGUEL MÚZQUIZ, MINISTER OF FINANCES

A pesar de inconvenientes, que son muchos, mi dictamen es que se
aprecie la composicion que nos ofrecen los Yngleses: que se dipute
Persona para tratar de ella; y que no se diga una palabra à los
Aliados hasta que se ponga en estado de que no la puedan deshacer.

el secreto es el alma de este negocio: Los Embajadores y Ministros
publicos nunca se han considerado a proposito para este genero de
negociaciones, porque estàn demasiado observados, y servidos de
domesticos venales y sospechosos sin que lo puedan remediar—Seria
mejor embiar un desconocido que fuese pratico de aquel Pais, y que
con el expecioso pretexto de facilitar el rescate de nuestras presas
tratase sin sospecho con los Ministros de Londres, sin perjuicio de
que los Ministros de pompa que el Rey quisiese autorizen con su
firma la convencion quando estèn acordados los articulos de ella.

Esta demonstracion de los Yngleses arguye un arrepentimiento
de avernos dado motivo a que entremos en la Guerra, variando el
modo de pensar que tenian en los años antecedentes: Las señas des-
monten el rezelo de que nos traten con doblez: Son los solicitantes:
estàn preocupados de que pueden triunfar de los Franceses quando
tienen la Guerra con ellos solos: Se hallan embarazados con los
cuidados que les aumenta la de España, privados del comercio util
que hacen con ella, dando lugar a que tome mas cuerpo el que hacen
sus Rivales. Estas y otras circunstancias no pueden dejar de entrar
en sus calculos.

Si fuese tal nr̃a desgracia que los Franceses penetren este negociacion antes de tiempo les serà facil eludirla, siendo nr̃a disculpa
legitima por la consideracion de que solo tratamos de oir los proposiciones con que nos han buscado los Yngleses para fiarselas
oportunamente segun nuestra buena fee; pero si se logra su buen

[1] Originals in AHN, *Est.* 4220, *Expdte.* 2, Docs. 13, 14, 15, 16. The first
opinion, which is unsigned, is presumably that of Múzquiz, Minister of
Finances. The Council meeting was held the evening of February 28, 1780.

exito solo tendrèmos que sufrir sus resentimientos de palabra, y las consequencias siempre seràn favorables para la España. Verà la Francia que quando llegue a faltarnos tenemos recursos à otras Potencias, è iràn conociendo que es equivocado el concepto de que les conviene tanto nuestra humillacion como la de los Yngleses por su comercio

el inconveniente mayor es el de que los Franceses pueden irritar contra nosotros à los Colonos; pero este temor se debileta con la persuasion en que estan los Yngleses de que compondràn derechamente y sin intervencion agena las diferencias que tienen con ellos concediendoles la independencia quando les acomode, y sobre todo el màl que nos resulta del abuso que hacen de nuestra sinceridad los Franceses no puede hacerse mayor, ni tan grande, con las consequencias de esta negociacion.

Nada toco de las Ynstrucciones que se han de dar al Comissionado porque el Ministro de Estado està perfectamente instruido de los intereses de la Monarquia, y de los puntos favorables que sean compatibles con la situacion de las cosas debiendo fiarse a su destroza y cuidado los pasos de esta negociacion

Indico pues lo que alcanzo con mas pureza de intencion y deseo del acierto que inteligencia. El Pardo a 29 de Febrero de 1780

OPINION OF JOSEPH DE GALVEZ, MINISTER FOR THE INDIES

Supuestos los hechos que han precedido con la Corte de Londres, devo ceñir mi dictamen à los tres puntos sig^{tes}. que son de la m^{or}. consecuencia.

Primero. Si conviene entrar en explicaciones de paz con el Gov^{no}. Britanico, ô rechazar la propuesta que ha hecho à este fin, desconfiando de su buena fé?

Segundo. Si en caso de entablar negociacion se deve comunicar aora à la Francia?

tercero. Quando y como se ha de participar à esta Potencia, no conviniendo hazerlo en el dia?

En q^{to}. al primero me parece, que pues el Gov^{no}. de Ynglaterra solicita componer sus diferen^{s}. con la España, no se conpromete el soverano decoro del Rey en oir sus proposiciones; y aunq^{e}. sp^{re} se deva recelar de aquella Potencia para tratarla con todas las cautelas posibles, no seria convn^{te}. cerrarla los oidos, ni tampoco confiar en sus explicaciones para disminuir un apice en los medios de hazer la guerra con todo el vigor posible, mayorm^{te}. haviendose ido su Escuadra de Gibraltar sin oposicion alguna de la nuestra.

Por lo que haze al seg^{do}. punto soy de sentir, que no conviene revelar aora el asunto à la Francia, por que esto frustraria la negociacion desde sus primeros pasos, y tal vez nos pusiera luego en los Empenos arriesgados que ha contraido esta Potencia con las Colonias Americanas sin noticia ni Anuencia del Rey, siguiendo entonces la Corte de Versalles su maxima antigua y constante de arrastrar la España à sus miras ambiciosas.

Verdad es, que podemos recelar del Gov^{no}. Britanico la felonia de manifestar à n^{ro} Alia[do] que tratamos con él sin su participacion para introducir la desconfianza y la discordia; pero tambien es cierto, que los Yngleses tienen con la Francia muchos motivos de odio desde que reconocio la independen^{a}. de las Colonias, que no son trascendentales à la España, y que no les conviene poner à esta Monarquia en la violenta necesidad de adoptar el partido de reconocer à sus primeros Enemigos los Colonos. Y en el caso de q^{e}. la Corte de Londres nos hiciera semejante traicion veria despues la de Francia que ella nos havia vuscado, y conoceria que el oir sus proposiciones con desconfianza y reserva por no cerrar las puertas à la conciliacion, dista mucho de convenirse con el Enemigo sin dar parte al Aliado, como la Francia misma lo ha hecho muchas vezes con nosotros, y lo ha repetido en este t$\bar{p}$o.

Y sobre el tercer punto de quando y como convendra hazer sabidora à la Francia de n^{ra} negociacion si llega à entablarse con la Ynglaterra, creo que no deve aventurarse el exito de ella, y que por lo mismo sera el t$\bar{p}$o oportuno q^{do}. la tengamos asegurada y no dudemos ya de concluirla. En el modo puede consistir que la corte de Versalles conozca no haver el Rey olvidado sus intereses proponiendola medios decorosos para su conciliacion con la de Londres, sin que falte esencialm^{te}. al empeño contraido con los Colonos. Y como esto lo han de proporcionar, en mi concepto, las explicaciones de los Yngleses, podra resolverse en vista de ellas el modo de participarlas à la Francia y proponerla al mismo t$\bar{p}$o los medios decorosos con que puede hazer la paz, respecto de que su tratado con las Colonias la da bastante margen para ello.

En suma, mi dictamen es, que S.M. se digne nombrar persona de la m^{or}. confianza y secreto que trate de ajustar una paz honrosa con el Rey Ynglaterra, redoblando al mismo t$\bar{p}$o nuestros esfuerzos

para continuar la guerra con el m^{or}. vigor. Que no se confie la
negociacion à la Francia hasta que se conceptue asegurada la conclusion de ella. Que entonces se la manifieste lo que convenga, proponiendola medios honestos y honrosos de conciliacion. Y que si no
quisiere adoptarlos, la dexe el Rey en su empeño pues lo contrajo
sin participacion ni consejo de S M.

El Pardo 29 de Febrero de 1780

JPH DE GALVEZ

OPINION OF COUNT DE RICLA, MINISTER OF WAR

Haviendo el Conde de Florida blanca en la Junta de Minros de ayer
noche expuesto à ella con la mayor claridad, y extension, los Antecedentes, Progresos, y estado actual de un Principio de Negociacion,
producida smpre de Ynstancias de la Ynglaterra, y con la condicion
de proponerla solo à nosotros en particular, ynstando por fin en el
Dia que se nombre por nra parte Sujeto Condecorado para con
alguna formalidad empezar á oyr, y Ventilar los Yntereses respectivos de dha Negociacion nos previno dieramos Cada uno de los
vocales nro Dictamen con la brevedad posible, reducido à tres Ques-
tiones; 1ª. decir si conviene Acceder à la ultima Ynstancia de nombrar Sugeto Condecorado, q^e. oyga, y dè principio à la Negociacion;
2ª. Si conviene comunicar à nro Aliado el estado del Dia en este
Asumpto; 3ª. Si quando en el Dia no se juzgue este Paso necesario,
y Conven^te; Quando ô en que tiempo Convendra enterarle del todo,
y Deviendome ceñir por la brevedad â decir mi Parecer sin exten-
derme à motivar sino lo preciso; Digo, Que â la 1ª. Juzgo indispensable convenir en lo q^e. se propone; porq^e. siendo solo oyr, y tratar
la materia; si es respecto á nosotros á nada nos empeña no haviendo
condicion de suspension de hostilidades por nra parte; Sucediendonos
este caso en un estado de la mayor atencion de los Yngleses, y q^e.
pueden rezelar de emvio considerable de nrās fuerzas de tierra, y
mar al centro de nrõs mas estimables y utiles Posesiones del Reyno
de Mexico, y sus Anexos; Y si es por lo que respeta à la Francia;
como podemos perjudicarla en oyr y tantear, si podemos convinar la
Conclusion de un empeño con beneficio nro, y suyo; Al 2º. Punto No
hallo preciso, ni que sea regular segun mi modo de pensar (talvez
con Error) que uno Comunique à otro Aliado, Amigo, ô Persona de
su mayor Consideracion Pensam^to. ô Ydea, que para darle forma pide
Comunicacion de dos Ynteresados, antes si me pareceria faltar à
la Prudencia si antes de trñpo la trasladarà à la Persona q^e. le
interesaba, y mas estimaba; en este Concepto Considero este Asunto;

y segun la relacion de los antecedentes parece que también piensa assi nῑo Aliado en casos de igual naturaleza; por lo que Soy de Dictamen en nada faltamos en no comunicarselo ahora â la Francia. 3ª. el antecedente Punto me inclina â que el tiempo de Comunicar la Negociacion â la Francia, es el que nos dexò traslucir aunqᵉ. no declaro el miῑro de estado segun comprehendí, que fue; quando la Negociacion ó Conferencia tuviera favorables resultas con provavilidad de Seguridades: En este estado de nada concluydo, y si solo consultado, el Conde de Florida blanca hara presente al Rey el tmp̃o y terminos de hazer la Abertura â su Aliado, y solo el puede hazerlo con Conocimᵗᵒ; siendo la resolucion del Rey en este Caso, y en todos la Regla, y Seguridad de nῑos Aciertos oy 29. de febᵒ. de 1780

El Conde de Ricla

OPINION OF MARQUIS GONZALEZ DE CASTEJON, MINISTER OF MARINE

Dictamen del Marqˢ Gonzalez de Castejon Secretario de estado de S.M. y del Despacho de Marina

Respeto a la Exposicion echa anoche en la Junta de los Ministros de Estado por el sᵒʳ Conde de Florida Blanca, de el estado en que se hallan actualmente los asumptos pendientes de estado que nos manifestó, i la tan critica, como precisa breuissima resolucion en el Dia, en los tres puntos Siguientes:

1º: Si Combendra abrir la Negociacion, que nos explicó en los terminos que se proporcionava, y de no haversido solicitada por S.M.— 2º Si deueria explicarse esta a nuestros aliados, 3º Y a que tiempo: expondre con la brevedad que el tiempo exije:—

Que me parece Combiene abrir la Negociacion, por hauer sido Solicitado S M para ella; por la uentajas que puedan resultar, segun el aspecto que manifieste su auertura, i las ocurrencia qᵉ las porcionen, quedando siempre, si asi no fuere en el arbitrio de no proseguirla.

Que no pudiendo aun Sauer el como ni con que Circunstancias, ni Ydeas se prouera esta auertura, hacerla a otros parece intempestibo, i aun manifestar un deseo que S M no ha tenido ni ha indicado, ademas de las fuertes razones que el Sᵒʳ conde de Florida Blanca expuso a la Junta en este mismo modo de opinar.

Que el Quando o a que tiempo, Solo puede graduarse Segun la auertura Sea, las proporciones qᵉ ofrezca, e Yncidentes, imposibles desde aora preverse, siendo preciso que concurran algunos, que aun entonces necessiten un mui reflexibo Examen para hacerlo.

Y q^e aora deuemos obrar con la maior actiuidad posible en la Guerra y sus preparatibos El Pardo 29 de febrero de 1780

El Marq^s Gonz^z de Castejon

NO. 4

THE SECOND SET OF JOHNSTONE'S PROPOSED PEACE ARTICLES AND
FLORIDABLANCA'S COMMENTS THEREON, *circa* March 1780[1]

NOTA

Este plan de Preliminares lo entregó el Comodore Johnstone en
Lisboa a D^n Luis Cantofer, sin embargo es la resp^{ta} q^e dimos antes
se mando entrar en materia. Dho cantofer la puso en manos de nr̃o
Embaj^{or} Conde de Fernannuñez y este la envió aqui con carta confidencial

En 2 de Marzo despachamos correo a dho Emb^{or} con otra confidencial del jefe y una especie de nota ô resp^{ta} a dhos Prelim^{es}; esto
es para gob^{no} de cantofer nò para entregarla a Johnstone; pero se
le incluyó pliego para dirijir a Lond al P^e Hussey por ser corre-
lativo del asunto: y al mismo se enviaron Duplicados por otros
conductos

Articles Preliminaire[s] pour Servir de Base aux Negociations
Entre L'Angleterre, L'Espagne et la France—

1

Les Colonies Anglaise de L'Amerique Septentrionale Continu-
eront dependant de la grande Bretagne, mais ils Seront intitulés a
toutes les privileges qui leurs ont eté offert par les Commissaires en
1778.

2

Une Garantie Mutuelle entre les puissances Beligerantes de leurs
divers Pocessions en Amerique, Auxquels La Cour de Portugal
Seroit Aussi invité d'Acceder comme un des partie—

---

[1] Originals in AHN, *Est.* 4220, *Expdte.* 2, Docs. 18, 19, 20. The first
document (No. 18) is a note by Campo, Floridablanca's secretary, explaining the origin of the articles, and the reply. The second document (No.
19) is the Johnstone articles. The third document (No. 20) contains
Floridablanca's comments in his own French. The fourth document (No. 21)
is a request by Floridablanca to Campo to put the comments into two
copies of good French, for further discussion.

3

Une Restauration Mutuelle des Places qui ont eté Conquis de part et d'Autre, En Europe Asie, Amerique et Afrique—

4

La Forteresse de Gibraltar Seroit rendû a Sa Majesté Catholique, Moyenant la Valeur des Munitions et Artilleries que l'on payeroit a L'Angleterre

5

Le Privilege de Pecher Sur le Banc de Terre Neuve, Assigné a la france par le Traité d'Utrecht, Seroit Egalement Ouverte aux Sujets de Sa Majesté Catholique dans ses Limites—

Le Traité de Paris feroit la Base de la presente Negociation—

1

Come le premier article n'è pas dans le pouvoir de S.M.C. l' on pourroit le proposer dans les termes suivants.

S.M.Cat^e. fera aupres les Colonies americaine et aupres la france toutes les demarches e les bons Ofices che lui seront proposés ou agreès par S.M.Brit^e. pour reduire celles-la a un accomodement onorable de part et autre capable de remplir les vües moderes de la susdite M.Britan^e.; e comme il i aura de tres gran difficultes a aplanir, qui demanderont dù tems, S.M.Britaniq^e. se chargerà de suivre la negociation avec les colonies et de la finir dans des termes et avec des stipulations que celles-ci n'aient pas de justes motifs de reclamer les secours stipulès entre la france, e les colonies dans le traite d'alliance eventuel di 6 febrier 1778; et pour i parvenir on acordera un Suspension de hostilites aux Colonies promettant toutes les autres belligerantes de ne se pas meler de cette negociation che dans le cas où S.M.Brit^e. leur proposroit ou demanderoit quelque ofice ou demarche.

2

La Garantie serà bornè aux poesions que resteront aux Puissances belligerantes par le traitè de Paix dont S'agit.

3

Il ni à rien a dire.

4

aceptè.

5

au lieu de cette cesion La Espagne voudroit celle della moitiè de la floride, en laissant aux anglois la partie oriental depuis l'embouchure du canal de Bahama au dehors, et en prenant la partie occidental au dedans du golfe de Mexique; et dans ce cas l'espagne donneroit quelque recompense si il en falloit a l'Angleterre.

6

il faut expliquer le traitè de Paris a l'egard della Bahie d'Honduras pour eviter de nouvelles demelès de ce cote-la en fixant d'un maniere claire l'autorite des Gouverneurs spagnols dans leurs territoires, pour faire obsrver la justice e la police aux Colones anglois etablis pour couper le bois de tinture, sous les precautionss necesaires pour empecher les vexations et les desordres—

7

On devroit ajouter un article où on stipuleroit:

Que dans le cas d'acceder S.M. tres cret. a ces preliminaires / on regleroit entre les deux cours de Versailles et Londres tout ce qui regarderoit aux interets et aux convenances des deux souverains et de leurs sujets respectifs; et S.M.Cat^e. feroit les ofices qui lui seroient agrees tous les deux./

En 2 di Marzo 1780
se envió al P^e Hussey esta nota
con la copia de los prelim^{es} pro-
puestos por Johnstone en Lisboa.

Sor D^n Bernardo saque Vm—una Copia del papelito de preliminares que embió fernan nuñez y a continuac^{on} copie Vm. mis adiciones articulo por articulo, enmendando solo alguna palabra o locuc^{on} q^e no sea francesa; bien entendido q^e es menor malo dejar alguna impropriedad que no variar, porq^e todo va puesto con estudio.

Necesito dos copias; y asi sacada la primera, se dedicara Vm. a la seg^{da}. y me las dara p^{ra}. esta noche o manaña. Despues hablaremos. Soi de Vm

MIERCOLES.

FLORIDABLANCA'S DISPATCHES TO HUSSEY, EL PARDO, FEBRUARY 29,
MARCH 2, MARCH 5, 1780, AUTHORIZING HIM UNDER CERTAIN
CONDITIONS TO ARRANGE THE PRELIMINARIES OF PEACE
BETWEEN ENGLAND AND SPAIN[1]

"NOTA

"en el mismo dia se envió el Duplicado de todo esto al mismo Hussey por
nro Embor en Lisboa reservadamte."

La carta de Vm. de 16 deste mes se reduce en substancia a que el
Gavinete britanico ha nombrado o nombrara un sugeto de su confianza para tratar con la España, en caso que esta quiera nombrar
otro, los quales procederan sobre la basa del tratado de Paris, y en
el curso de la negociacion podran entrar en materia sobre la evacuacion o cambio de Gibraltar; añadiendo que al fin verà el mundo
quan sinceramente desea S.M.Brit^ca. la Paz con la España.

He dado quenta al Rey desta nueva abentura del Ministerio ingles,
y aunque S. Mag^d. no vè en ella mas que ambiguedades y restric-
ciones, quando el modo de acercarse sinceramente a la reconcilia-
cion era la franqueza y claridad que forman el Caracter del Rey,
y que deberian ser la regla de ambos gavinetes; sin embargo S.M.
hà mandado examinar la materia con la mayor brebedad, y avisare
a Vm. de las resultas de este examen: bien entendido que si ese
Ministerio no està dispuesto a salvar el decoro de S. Mag^d. con sin-

[1] Originals in AHN, *Est.* 4220, *Expdte.* 2, Docs. 99, 94, 101. The letters
of February 29 and March 2, 1780 (Documents 99 and 94) were written
and signed by Floridablanca. There is also a copy in Campo's hand of that
of March 2 (Document 93), endorsed as follows:

"El Pardo 2 de Marzo de 1780

"A Don Tomas Hussey

"Debolviandole su criado el qual debe embarcarse en la Coruña, Oporto
ô donde mejor se le proporcione

"Se contesta a su expedon de 16 de Febo y se le explica el modo de pensar
del Rei en asunto al projectado ajuste de paz.

"Se le remite la copia de un plan de Preliminares qe nos ha venido por
Lisboa suponiendo ser propuesta del Gavte Britco y de una respta a ellos.

The letter of March 5, 1780, sent by way of The Hague (Document 101)
is in Campo's hand. In the cipher (Document 102) it is slightly abridged.
It has not seemed worthwhile to reproduce the translated cipher here.

ceridad y buena fè, y no contribuye a que no se pierdan los in-
stantes; ni Yo podré detener el curso de las negociaciones del S^or.
Jai que està yà en camino para Madrid, ni los proyectos que estan
concebidos, y en que se trabaja con la mayor actividad: De modo
que a pesar de mis buenos deseos podran empeorarse las cosas, y
solo serviran estos manejos de eternizar la guerra a que estamos re-
sueltos hasta dar el ultimo suspiro, si se nos cree engañar, seducir,
o entretener con dilaciones y vagas esperanzas. Dios g^e a Vm. m^os.
a^os como des^o. Pardo 29 de feb^ro. de 1780

El Conde de floridablanca

S^or D^n. thomas Husei

Me ha llegado el aviso que Vm. me dà en carta de 16 de febrero
sobre las disposiciones de esa corte para nombrar una Persona, que
con otra que nombre el rey n^ro S^or. entablen y concluyan una negociacion de Paz; diciendo ese Ministerio que al mismo tiempo se
podra tratar de la cesion y cambio de Gibraltar, y que al fin verà
el Mundo si la Ynglaterra desea sinceramente la Paz con la España.
Supone Vm. que el tratado há de ser sobre la basa del de Paris; y
no se atreve Vm. a adelantar congeturas bien fundadas sobre la
extension que dara esa corte a sus disposiciones pacificas y gene-
rosas para con nosotros.

Al mismo tiempo que la citada carta de Vm. me ha venido por la
via de Lisboa una nota de Preliminares, que se supone conforme a
las intenciones de la Corte de Londres para explorar las nuestras.
Remito a Vm. una copia de dicha nota y al margen de ella verà Vm.
las adiciones, y explicaciones que se han puesto con las quales podria
concluirse desde luego esta negociacion; sirviendo a Vm. de regla
dichas explicaciones marginales, q^e aceptadas, podrian formalizarse
en Lisboa, entre nuestro Embaxador y el Ministro o Persona que
nombrase la Ynglaterra: en su defecto podrian evacuarse las formalidades del tratado en la Haya; y si absolutam^te. se queria que
fuese en Londres buscariamos persona para ello: Pero desde luego
està Vm. autorizado para tratar y concluir esta negociacion, reser-
vando solo las formalidades exteriores para las personas y en los
Parages que llevo insinuados.

Como Vm està enterado de la recompensa que dariamos, si fuese
necesaria para concluir, escuso entrar en otras discusiones: solo
añado que si ocurrieren algunas dudas pueden quedar reservadas a

los que fenescan y extendian el tratado en Lisboa, donde avrà mas facilidad de negociar con brebedad, y secreto; a cuyo fin avra alli persona bien intencionada, e indiferente, que concluya la negociacion hasta hallarse en estado de recibir la ultima formalidad.

Entretanto digo a Vm. que de un dia a otro llegara el S^{or}. Jai Diput^{do}. del Congreso, que salio yà de Cadiz para Madrid, y Yo no tendre arbitrio para detener largo tiempo su negociacion: conque esos Señores no deben perderlo en quedar dentro o fuera con la nuestra. tambien digo a Vm. y repito lo que le tengo escrito por la via de Lisboa, por donde recibira Vm. un Duplicado deste Despacho. En una palabra, si alguna Persona no bien intencionada piensa abusar de la bondad del Rey con dilaciones y artificios que no son presumibles, se equivacarà mucho, porque ni afloxamos un punto de n^{r}os preparativos, ni apesar de qualesquiera acacim^{tos}. somos capaces de faltar a nuestro honor, ni de recibir contra él la lei de n^{r}os enemigos, amigos, ni neutrales. Salvando pues el decoro de S.Mag^{d}. verà tambien la Ynglaterra quanto va a ganar en su Paz con la España, y en cultivar para lo succesivo nuestra amistad y union de que resultaran muchas ventajas a los subdn^{tos} de ambas coronas. Dios g^{e} a Vm m^{os}. a^{os}. como des^{o}.

Pardo 2 de Marzo de 1780.

El Conde de Floridablanca

S^{or} D^{n}. thomas Husei.

En el Pardo a 5 de Marzo 1780—a d^{n} Tomas Hussey en cifra y se enviò por mano de n^{r}o Mn^{r}o en Hol^{da} con motivo de Despacharle correo por el nacim^{to} del Infante.

Llego el criado de Vm y me entregó su despacho en que no hallo de parte de esa corte toda la claridad y abertura necesarias para adelantar la conclusion del negocio como a todos conviene.

Al mismo tiempo me ha venido por Lisboa un plan de Preliminares y pienso escribir a Vm̃ por aquella via extensam^{te} communicandoselo y dando nuestras observaciones sobre èl. Entretanto para ganar tiempo y que Vm̃ haga uso de ello voi a referirle los articulos que nos proponen y al pie de cada uno nr̃a observacion. Si ahi van di buena fè y quieren la paz, bastante autorizado esta Vm̃ paraq^{e} arreglar con èl los puntos principales: pues asegurado, esto luego se destinarà Persona nuestra que vaya a Lisboa a abocarse con la que venga di Londres para extender con formalidad y firmar los Pre-

liminares. Proposiciones venidas por Portugal. articulo primero. Las
colonias subsistiran dependientes de la Gran Bretaña pero des-
frutaran todos los privilegios q^e se las ofrecieron por los Comisarios
en el año de 1778. resp^{ta}. Como esto no depende de la España se
pondra en lugar de ella q^e S.M.C. hara los pasos y oficios q^e proponga S.M.B. para proporcionar un acomodam^{to} honroso con ellas
que sea adaptable a las miras moderadas de la Inglat^a; y como las
dificultades q^e puedan encontrarse exijirian demasiado tiempo ofrece
SMB. seguir la negociacion en tales terminos q^e no precise a las
Colonias a pedir a la Francia los socorros convenidos por su trat^o y
a este efecto establecer con ellas una suspension de hostilidades:
prometiendo las demas Potencias no mesclarse de tal negociacion
a menos q^e lo exija el Rei Brit^{co}. Segundo. Habra una garantia
mutua entre las Potencias beliger^{tes} de sus respectivas poses' en
America y se combidarà tambien al Portugal a acceder. Resp^{ta}: La
garantia se entenderà de las poses' segun se estipulan en el trat^o q^e
ahora se proyecta Tercero. Restitucion reciproca de todo lo q^e
por cada parte se haya conquistado en las quatro partes del
Mundo. Resp^{ta}. No hai reparo. Quatro. La cesion de Gibraltar
pagando los enseres a la Inglaterra. Resp^{ta}. Se acepta. Quinto.
Se extendera a los Españoles, en los limites q^e se señalaran,
la pesca en Terranova q^e gozan los franceses por el Trat^o de utrech.
Resp^{ta} En vez de esta cesion desea la Esp^a aquella parte de la
Florida q^e mira al Golfo de Mexico quedando a los Ingleses la parte
oriental: y en caso necesario no se negaria a dar alg^a compensacion
ó recompensa. Sexto. El Trat^o de Paris servira de basa de la pres^{te}
negociacion Resp^{ta}. Debe explicarse este trat^o en qu^{to} a los estab-
licim^{tos} de la Bahia de Honduras, de modo q^e se corten para sp$\bar{r}$e
las disputas, formandose los colonos en Poblaciones para su corte
de palo de tinto, q^e es lo unic^a q^e tienen derecho, bajo la direccion
y autor^d de Gobern^{es} españoles, y supuestas aquellas reservas y
preceden^s q^e convengan a unos y a otros. Un septimo articulo crea
preciso la España y es: Que si accede el Rei Crist^{mo} a estos Preliminares las cortes de Versalles y Londres reglarán los puntos q^e
las convengan y interesen particularm^{te}: ofreciendo SMC. pasar
los oficios amistosos q'ambas crean necesarios.

Si como se nos asegura de Lisboa acaba de enviar esa corte por
via de instrucc^{on} tales capitulos ya vé V$\tilde{m}$ que no sera dificil accelerar
un ajuste, p^s las variaciones q^e proponemos son justas y nada per-

judiciales a la Inglaterra. Reflexione Vm̃ sin embargo y haga re-
flexionar a esos S^es que mientras mas nos internemos en la campaña
mas se dificultan las cosas.

No escriba Vm̃ por Francia ni envie persona q^e se haga sospechosa

NO. 6

FLORIDABLANCA'S PLAN FOR PUBLIC AND SECRET TREATIES OF PEACE
BETWEEN GREAT BRITAIN AND SPAIN, *circa* March 1780[1]

Minuta para servir de Instruccion y tambien de plan de Tratados

Está a media margen por si a V.E.se le ocurre todavia algo que añadir y acompaña una esquelita con una nota

El Sujeto que hubiera de tratar con el Ministerio Brit^{co} sobre un ajuste entre las Coronas de Esp^a y Inglaterra deberia fijarse en los principios y reflexiones que se deducen de los Capitulos sig^{tes}: tomandolos por norma para un Tratado ô unos Preliminares, con cuya mira se extienden aqui bajo de aquel metodo.

Deseosos los Reyes Cat^{co} y Brit^{co} de contribuir con la mayor eficacia al restablicim^{to} de la quietud de Europa y a la segur^d de la navegacion y comerico q^e se han interrumpido y alterado con la pres^{te} Guerra en perjuicio de todas las Naciones; mirando ahora por el bien general de ellas y por el particular de sus propios Vasallos, los de sus Aliados y Amigos se han convenido en preparar la grande obra de la paz por medio de los articulos Preliminares q^e siguen.

1°

NOTA
en lugar de esto
p u e d e establecerse la cesacion
d e hostilidades
con anticip^{on} de
dos Meses al
cange de ratific^s.

Desde q^e se efectue el cange de las ratificaciones del pres^{te} Convenio habra una entera y absoluta cesacion de hostilid^{es} entre los respectivos subditos de S^s.M^{s}Cat^{ca} y Brit^{ca} asi por mar como por tierra en todos sus respectivos Dominios en las 4 partes del Mundo

---

[1] Original in AHN, *Est.* 4220, *Expdte.* 2, Doc. 98. The first draft (Document 97) is in Floridablanca's own handwriting. The document here reproduced is from a fair copy (Document 98) by Campo. On the Campo copy an archivist has written "Febrero 1780." The Floridablanca draft is preceded by a note in Campo's hand: "Esta Minuta del Gefe se ha puesto mas en claro a media margen para poner lo q^e falta y se ha entreg^{do} al Gefe quien la tiene en su poder, sin q^e hasta ahora se haya enviado. Es verdad q^e han venido por Lisboa mas proposic y se responde a ellas Marzo 2 de 1780"

2º

Dha cesacion se verificarà por lo tocante a Europa en el termino
de quince dias, ô antes sī los Generales, Comand^{tes} y Gobern^{es}
recibieren las ordenes ô noticias de este Tratado: por lo respectivo
a America y Africa dentro de quatro Meses; y dentro de ocho ô de
un año quando mas por lo coresp^{te} al Asia é India oriental; si
antes no hubiesen llegado las ordenes ô noticias de dho Tratado y
Articulos a los Gefes respectivos de mar y tierra en aquellas dis-
tancias: Debiendose advertir con este motivo q^e todas las presas
que se hicieren en el tp̄o intermedio desd[^e] cange de las ratificaciones se restituirán por ambas partes de buena fé

3

Todas las Plazas, Fortalezas y territorios q^e se hubieren ocupado
durantė la pres^{te} guerra en qualquiera parte del Mundo por una
de las dos Potencias referidas desposeyendo a la otra, se restituiran
reciprocam^{te} en los tiempos señalados en el articulo anterior;
igualm^{te} q^e su artilleria y pertrechos segun estaban al momento de
su ocupacion.

4º

De la regla anteced^{te} se exceptuan los Fuertes   x con la priv-
Plazas y Territorios de la Florida occidental y   ativa navegacion
todos los demas comprehendidos desde la em-   de dhos rios para
bocadura del Rio de S Mateo ō Sⁿ Juan en la misma Florida
mas al Norte del Fuerte de Sⁿ Agustin hasta dar buelta por
toda la costa del seno mexicano Panzacola y subir a las margenes
mas elevadas del Rio Misisipi en q^e se le incorporan los rios Misuri
Iberville y otros denomin^{os} diversam^{te} en las Cartas maritimas:
cuyas posesiones y territorios, (inclusos los q^e esten todavia en
poder de la Inglaterra dentro de dhos terminos) cede y ofrece
garantir perpetuam^{te} S.M.B.^{ca} al Rei Cat^{co} sus herederos y
Sucesores^x: asi como S.M.Cat^{ca} no solo renuncia todos y qualesquiera derechos y pretensiones a la Florida oriental, sus pertenencias
y territorios, ratificando la cesion hecha por el Trat^o de Paris de
10 de Marzo de 1763; sino q^e ademas ofrece tambien la perpetua
garantia de ellas a S.M.B^{ca}.

5

Para evitar las continuas discordias q^e han ocurrido y pueden repetirse entre los Subditos de las dos Coronas con motivo de los Establecim^tos Ingleses de la Bahia de Honduras y Costa de Campeche, no solo se arreglarán los Vasallos del Rei Brit^co a lo estipulado en el Art° 17 del mismo Trat° de Paris del 1763, sino que en donde se hubiera reunido aquellos establecim^tos en forma de poblacion habran de tener una Cabesa ō Gobern^or español, con los oficiales de gobierno Justicia y policia de q^e tubiere por conven^te S.M.C^ca, cuyos Vasallos podran establecerse alli en los mismos terminos: y las Casas ō establecimientos dispersos q^e actualm^te hubiere se asiguarán al territorio y dependencia de las respectivas Poblaciones q^e como es dicho han de tener Gob^or. En consecuencia de ello se recojerán qualesquiera nombram^tos ō Patentes q^e a nombre de S.M.B^ca se hubieren dado en aquellos Paises, ya sea a Europeos ō a Indios, para mandar y gobernar en los referidos establecim^tos.

6

En lo succesivo qualquier subdito del Rei Brit^co que quisiere establecer su casa ō almacenes en aquellos parages para el corte del palo de tinto, q^e es el unico derecho que se ha concedido en ellos a la Nacion Inglesa: debera dar cuenta al Gob^or ô Gefe español del territorio ô sitio de la costa donde se quiera fijar: bajo las reglas y precauc^s corresp^tes para evitar los abusos opuestos a dho Trat° y de los anteriores. No preced^do este requista podra y debera ser expelido qualquier sujeto q^e se intente establecer en dhos parages: y se advierte q^e tampoco ha de servir el pretexto del corte del palo paraq^e los Ingleses se introduscan en las Prov^as y Poblaciones españolas.

7

Todas las Presas y vejaciones hechas por la marina Inglesa a los vasallos y Pavellon de SM.C^ca antes de declarar la pres^te Guerra, cuya epoca se fijará en el dia 21 de Junio de 1779, se examinarán de buenafé por dos Comisarios q^e han de nombrar ambas Cortes y se decidiran por ellos dentro del termino de los seis Meses siguientes a la rat^on de estos Preliminares: de suerte q^e lo q^e se resuelban en punto de indemnisacion y satisfacc^on a las partes agraviadas, se egecutará sin replica, discusion ni retardo alg°.

El Tratado publico podria ceñirse a los puntos q^e van especificados por ser conformes a razon y a equidad; pero como hai otros que no interesan menos a la Esp^a y a cuyo arreglo se juzga acreedora por muchos motivos, se procede ahora a indicarlos para qᵉ se extiendan en Tratado secreto: Bien entendido qᵉ ambos se han de ajustar y firmar en un dia mismo y qᵉ el uno no sera valido sin el otro: cuyo Tratado secreto podria denominarse *convencion de cambio, trueque ō permuta*

En consideracion a los perjuicios padecidos en la presᵗᵉ Guerra y a los enormes gastos y armamᵗᵒˢ que se vió obligada a hacer la corona de Espᵃ, para impedir el progreso de los abusos de la Marina Inglesa, de qᵉ se hace clara mencion en el artº 7º del tratado publico firmado en este mismo dia; como tambien con el fin de afirmar perpetuamᵗᵉ una verdadera amistad entre las dos Naciones española y Inglesa, arrancando las raices de toda emulacion enemistad y discordia: se han convenido los Sobⁿᵒˢ de Espᵃ y de la Gran Bretaña en qᵉ S.M.B.ᶜᵃ cederia, como de presᵗᵉ cede, a S.M.Catᶜᵃ sus Herederos y Sucesores, las Plazas de Gibraltar y Menorca, con todos sus derechos y pertenencias en la misma forma que fueron cedidas a la Inglaterra por los artºˢ *10* y *11* del Tratº de Utrech de 1713: y se verificara la entrega de estas Fortalezas a los quince dias despˢ del cange de las ratificacˢ de la presᵗᵉ Convencion

NOTA

Que debe servir para hacer conocer al Ministo Britᶜᵒ la necesᵈ de este artº lo.

Gibraltar y Menorca son dos objetos qᵉ tiene la Espᵃ tan a la vista qᵉ jamas podra olvidarlos. No es posible qᵉ la Nacion española se reconcilie perpetue y cordialmᵗᵉ con la Inglesa mientras no se halle el modo de apartar de la vista aquellos dos monumentos de disgusto y de enemistad entre ambas.

La ciudad de Oran y el Ptº de Maralquivir ofrecen a la Corte de Londres el mejor fondeadero de la costa de Africa y una Plaza bien fortificada para hacer desde ella todo el comercio de aquella parte de Berberia, extendiendose a los terrenos y cultivos qᵉ la España no puede desfrutar. Si S.M.B. compara con esto el esteril peñasco de Gibraltar y el costoso establecimᵗᵒ de Mahon verá que vá a gañar mucho, conservando los mismos ō mejores puntos de apoyo que ahora tiene en el Mediterraneo.

Lo que va expuesto es con relacion al segᵈᵒ articulo qᵉ se pone ofreciendo la Espᵃ aquellas Plazas; pero esto es para el ultimo extremo: pˢ el deseo principal es lograr la restitucion de Gibraltar sin trueque algº. Si absolutamᵗᵉ se niega a ello Gavinete Britᶜᵒ y por otro lado cede a Mahon con Gibraltar en el supᵗᵒ de qᵉ haya remuneracion, en tal caso entra dho 2º artº con la oferta de Oran y Maralquivir

Art° 2°

Por una especie de compensacion y señal de gratitud de parte de S.M.C^{ca} a la cesion anteced^{te}, cede desde luego a S.M.B., sus Herederos y Succesores, las Plazas de Oran y Maralquivir con su respectivo Puerto: cuya entrega se efectuará en iguales terminos q^e la expresada en el cap° anterior.

3

NOTA
Debe entender-
se q^e este Art°
3° tendra ca-
bim^{to} q u a n d o
haya sido indis-
pensable poner
el seg^{do}

Se nombraran Comisarios por ambas Partes q^e formando los Inventarios y valuaciones de la Artilleria y Pertrechos de ambas cesiones, regulen el importe de modo q^e se pague en dinero efectivo sin el menor retardo el exceso q^e hubiere de una parte o de otra.

4

Habiendo dado motivo a la pres^{te} Guerra las desconfianzas causadas entre la corte de Lond^s y otras, y señaladam^{te} con las de Esp^a y Francia de resultas de las turbac^s q^e se suscitavan y subsisten entre la Gran Bretaña y sus antiguas Colonias del Contin^{te} de la America Septentrional: Han resuelto S^s M^s Cat^{ca} y Brit^{ca} poner de comun acuerdo todos los medios posibles para extinguir las expresadas turbaciones ō guerra efectiva con las mismas Colonias; y a este fin se han convenido en combidar a S:M.Crist^{ma} a acceder a la suspension de hostilidades y restit^{on} pactada en los Art^{os} del Tratado publico

5

Supuesto la accesion del Rei Crist^{mo} se reserva S.M.B^{ca} tratar con la corte de Versalles de sus respectivos y reciprocos intereses: mediando tambien en ello, si se juzga del caso, el Rei Cat°.

6

NOTA
La Francia se
obligó a no de-
jar las armas
hasta q^e fuese re-
conocida la in-
dependencia *ex-
presa ō taci-*

Mediante hallarse ya S.MB. enterado de q^e el Tratado de alianza y reconocim^{to} de la Independencia de las Colonias ajustado por la Francia en 6 de Feb° de 1778 fué eventual y condicional para el caso en q^e la Inglaterra declarase la guerra a la Francia; y q^e por consig^{te} la fuerza de los empeños de aquel Trat° (a que segun se tiene entend° no faltará jamas el Rei Crist^{mo}) viene a depender de la misma Guerra, aunq^e esta ha procedido de hecho por via de represalias y sin formal declaracion: con tales antecedentes toma a su cargo el mismo Rei Brit^{co}, en caso de acceder S.M.C^{ma} al Tratado arriba dho, concertarse con las colonias en terminos q^e no puedan justam^{te} reclamar ni reconvenir a la Francia sobre los Pactos de dha alianza: a cuyo fin las concederá S.M.B. desde luego una suspension de hostilidades, y para estos casos ofrecerá el Rei Crist^{mo} no mezclarse directa ni indirectam^{te} en el concierto y sus consecuencias.

tam^{te}. Las palabras puestas en este art° 6°. y rayadas parece q^e son un reconocm^{to} tacito y aun expreso: una vez que el concierto ha de ser en terminos q^e no puedan justam^{te} *reclamar la alianza*, la q^e podrian reclamar sino fuesen reconocidas

7

Por amor de la paz y de la Humanidad se reserva unicam^{te} el Rei Cat^{co} el cuidado de pasar sus oficios amistosos para dhos ajustes en el caso de q^e sean gratos a todas las Potencias beligerantes: como en efecto los ha pasado y repite para recomendar a la espiritu magnanimo del Rei de la Gran Bretaña la buena suerte de las Colonias. Y en caso de no ser gratos dhos oficios ofrece S.M.Cat^a desde luego no mezclarse directa ni indirectam^{te} en estos asuntos; ni tomar parte en las desvenencias q^e pudieren causar. A lo dicho se reducen substancialm^{te} los dos Tratados q^e se proponen y el Sujeto a quien se ha de fiar tan importante encargo deve tener sp̃re a la vista q^e sino se concluyen mui luego no se concluiran jamas: Que si se dá tiempo a que empiezen las operac^s de la prop^a Campaña, la cual verosimilm^{te} será mui viva, cada dia se imposibilitará mas el Negocio: Que la tardanza, por corta q^e sea, ha de producir desconfianzas de ambas partes, ha de dar lugar a q^e se descubra la negociacion y finalm^{te} ha de causar nuevos embarazos quando es notorio q^e está ya en España y llegará un dia de estos a Madrid el Ministro del Congreso Americano destinado a esta Corte.

El Art°. 4 q^e trata de la Florida puede presentar alguna duda, Primero se dice q^e nos ha de ceder la Inglaterra desde el rio Sⁿ Juan enfrente del canal Bahama hasta todo el rio Misisipi en lo qual se comprehenden Sⁿ Agⁿ, Panzacola y toda aquella costa. Desp^s concluye con que garantiremos a la misma Inglat^a lo q^e se la asignó en el Tratado de Paris, q^e es asimismo S^n Ag^n, Panzacola &c. Escusando las voces Florida oriental y Florida occidental y poniendo especificam^{te} lo q^e pedimos ahora parece q^e se salvan a la equivocacion: sobre todo si se tiene cuidado de no especificar lo q^e quede a la Inglat^a sino con expresion generica como *todo lo restante. &c*

The first relay will meet you at Badajox the Frontier town of
Spain; at an Inn called, the *Posada de la Soledad,* & will carry you
to Merida where you will Stop to refresh it is [figure cut off] leagues
from Badajox from thence you will go to sleep in R [?] iajada 8
leagues further, & stop at a neat little Spanish Inn called *Posada
nueva, frente de la carcel.* Here you will meet with a 2^d Relay which
will carry you to Truxillo to refresh, & afterwards to *Venta del
lugar nuevo* to lie—on the Banks of the Tagus, where you will find
plenty of [f]ish, & in the most romantic spot I ever saw. This is the
place where the 3^d. Relay is ordered to meet you, & will carry you
to dinner (or to refresh) to *la Calzada* 7 leagues & to sleep at Talavera la Reina. Here a 4 Relay meets you & carrys you to refresh
at a little village near Toledo, & to stop here at Aranjuez *WHERE
EVERY THING ELSE,* as well as my heart, will be ready to receive
you, & your familly. The road, all the way, is very good, except during
three leagues on this side of *Truxillo,* where it becomes steepy &
hilly & continues so 3 leagues untill you come to *Venta del lugar*
nuevo mentioned in this Meṁ: all the rest of the road is very good.
You will carry your bedding with you, & buy in Lisbon four little
portable canvas bedst^{ds}: Send all your baggage (except such as you
will want to dress in iṁediately on your arrival here) either by
mules, or in a Calash, with, or without a Servant: for the Relays
will not carry all your baggage. The Coaches you will meet can contain yourself, the three Ladies, & maid. The other two Servants
may go on the outside. Travel always from 5 in the evening untill
eleven the following morning: otherwise the heat may have a bad
effect on you & let your time for sleep be from 11: in the morn^g
till 5 in the evening. There is not the least danger from highway
men on the road. I have made Daly my market man on the road, that
he might qualify himself to be the more usefull to you. Take care
however always to have *some* provisions in the Coach, in case of

1 Original in R.O., S.P.F., Series 94, Vol. 209.

not being able to meet with any in the Villages thro' which you pass. Besides Tea & its appurtenances you will bring with you a few plates, knives & forks—table linen—a few wax candles & candlesticks: in short, every thing you should want if you were to lodge in an empty barn. The Moment Daly reaches you, send off a relay to *Estremos,* a little town within 8 leagues of the Frontiers of Spain, from whence it is to carry you to Badajos—in six hours after send another to wait for you at *Silveira,* which will carry you to *Estremos*: & the following day send of a third to Aldea Gallega, which will carry you to Silveira which is twelve leagues. This will enable you to go from Lisbon to Badajos in a day & a half, & the Relays I send will bring you in four days more to this Court. It is unnecessary to tell you with what impatience I wait your arrival —to see once more my dearest Friends, & to tell you a 1000 things which *I do not write.* As you come along mark down without loss of time, (on the spot) the observations you happen to make—Everything will appear much more new, & singular to you, than it could to me who had seen the same things before in my youth write to me from Lisbon & once or twice on the road & put your letter under cover, & on the outside to S^r. D^n: Bernardo del Campo—Aranjuez. This will be the best way at present for the letter to reach me. Endorsed:

In Mr Hussey's to
Mr Cumberland 24 May 1780
In D^{ls}. N 2.

FLORIDABLANCA'S MEMORANDUM DELIVERED TO HUSSEY AND ORALLY
TRANSLATED BY THE LATTER TO CUMBERLAND AT ARANJUEZ,
circa JUNE 18, 1780[1]

Quando Yo vine a Madrid en principios de Enero deste año, me
parecio que este Gavinete no huviera repugnado una negociacion de
Paz manejada, en los terminos que comunique al Lord Germaine.
Sin embargo noté que el Ministerio español estaba mui desconfiado
del Ministerio de Londres talvez porque presumiese que con las
voces y aberturas q^e se esparcian p^r Lisboa y otras partes procura-
bamos adormecerle, para dar algunas golpes a la España en sus
posesiones de America o indisponerle con la francia. En aquel tiempo
y carta q^e escribi a Milord Germaine dije que qualquier negociacion
q^e se lograse abrir debia seguirse y fenecerse en todo febrero, porque
se estaba esperando de un dia a otro un Ministro del Congreso
americano, y podrian obligar las circunstancias a contraher algun
empeño con el, en cuyo caso, seria ya imposible llevar adelante la
negociacion, y romper el empeño que se huviese tomado.

Bolvi a Londres con las luces que adquiri, y en este intervalo
sufriò la España el descalabro de la Escuadra de Langara, y socorro de Gibraltar. tambien arrivo a Cadiz y despues a Madrid el
Minřo del Congreso Monsr. Jai, con su Sec^{r10} y adjunto Monsr de
Caimichael. El golpe dado a Langara lejos de poner nuestra negociacion de mejor aspecto la empeorò; porque comenzo a creer mas
fuertemente el Ministerio español, que la Inglaterra no usaria desta
y otras aberturas de negociacion, sino para introducir algun descuido
en las operaciones de la Campaña y aprovecharse del tiempo para
algunas expediciones o conquistas en America; y efectivamente
parece segun hà mostrado la experiencia, que desde entonces se
dedicò la corte de Madrid con mayor actividad a despachar la grande

---

[1] Original in AHN, *Est.* 4220, *Expdte.* 2, Doc. 67. The document here
reproduced—mentioned in the text of Chapter VI, above, as the "political
memorandum" in contradistinction from the "travel memorandum"—is a
draft in Floridablanca's own hand. There is also a copy (Document 68) in
Hussey's hand.

expedicion que salio de Cadiz en 28 de Abril, la qual huviera salido como he oido en principios del mismo mes, si algunos accidentes no la huviesen retardado.

A esta novedad se agregaron otras muchos, como la llegada del Conde de Guichen a la Martinica; la noticia de las desgracias padecidas en su navegacion por el Grāl Clinton; la recuperacion del fuerte de Omoa en Honduras; la salida y destrucc.^{on} de los establecimientos ingleses en aquella Bahia y costa de Campeche; los progresos que se creen aqui hechos en la conquista de la Florida; la feliz salida de Brest de la expedicion del Cavallero de Ternaij; las esperanzas que dan todas estas combinaciones, el ningun recelo q^e ya se tiene de q^e en este año ayan podido imvadirse las islas filipinas, visto el mal estado en q^e el Almir^{te} Hughes existia el 4 de Noviembre del año pasado en la Bahia de las tablas y finalmente las instancias y promesas vigorosas que hacen aqui los Diput^{dos}, americanos. todas estas cosas ocurridas desp^s. de mi primera viage, han aumentado las dificulta^{es} p^{ra} emprehender aqui una negociacion favorable, por mas buenas intenciones que tengà este Soberano el qual segun todas mis noticias ciertamente desea, o Yo me engaño mucho, hallar algun medio honorifico y decente de dar la Paz a la Europa. el caracter humano compasivo y religioso deste Principe lo conducen por si mismo a aquel deseo, pero su natural firmeza y pundonor, que algunos graduan de teson extraordinario, impiden la flexibilidad en muchos puntos, especialm^{te} si S.M.cree que pueden ser contra su decoro, o los empeños de su palabra y obligaciones.

A pesar de tan dificil situacion he procurado tantear este Ministerio, y hallo que los puntos cardinales de las dificultades grandes del dia pueden ser tres: 1° sobre el modo de negociar incluyendo o excluyendo a la franc^a. de la negociac^{on}: 2°. sobre el modo de comprehender o excluir a las Colonias: 3 sobre ceder o no la Plaza de Gibraltar. Dire el juicio q^e formo en cada uno destos tres puntos, deducido de las conferencias q^e he tenido, de las Observaciones que he hecho, y de los raciocinios y conjeturas que he formado lleno de zelo, y de un deseo fervoroso de la Paz y del bien de ambas Naziones y Monarchias.

Por lo que mira al primer punto, no parece imposible que la España se preste a un tratado separado con la Inglaterra, y que en el dia abandone a la francia. El Caracter honrado, y pundonoroso del Rey de españa impide que se le pueda mover a un paso que chocaria con sus principios. Por otra parte la Politica de su Ministerio no se fiaria mucho de las promesas de la Inglaterra; y creeria que el designio desta seria enredar la España con la franc^a. introduciendo desconfianzas. Ademas desto las ofertas que aqui podemos hacer no parece que llevan las ideas, ni los deseos de esta Corte, para inclinarla a desviarse de su Antiguo aliado. Los resentim^{tos}. de la España con la francia no son bastantes, paraque se arroje a dejar a esta por la Inglaterra, de quien dice no tener hasta aora Seguridad alg^{na}. ni esperanza de graves utilidades. Si la Inglaterra huviera aprovechado los momentos fuertes y vibos de aquel resentimiento, tanto al tiempo de hacer y publicar la franc^a su trat^{do}. con el Cong^{so}. americano, quanto al tiempo del golpe de Gibraltar, podria talvez la corte de Londres aver sacado Partido, y abierto la Puerta a grandes sucesos; pero se dejaron pasar aquellas ocasiones, y crecieron con la tardanza las desconfianzas, y las dificultades apuntadas arriba.

Es mucho mas dificil dho tratado separado, si se considera, que ya se ha hecho publica en Lisboa y aun en Paris, segun las ultimas Cartas recibidas alli de Londres la venida del Cav^{ro}. Cumberland, y la sospecha de q^e trahiga algun encargo relativo a la Paz. Por mas que se aya echado la especie de aver venido a recuperar la salud de su fam^{lia}, que pasa a Italia, y que quando mas se detendra a arreglar un cartel de cange de prisioneros, las sospechas de la Corte de Paris, sus Espias, y sus apasion^{dos}. en esta corte han de poner al Ministerio español en la sugecion y en la necesidad de no ocultar esta negociacion a los franceses; y en tales circumstancias es imposible que se entable y tenga efecto un tratado separado.

el Ministerio español ha sospechado que esta publicidad es artificiosam^{te}. dispuesta por el Ministerio ingles para introducir la discordia entre las cortes de Madrid y Versalles; y desconfiar a las Colonias; porq^e en el instante que llegamos a Lisboa, explicò el Comodoro Jonston con señas individuales todo el asunto de nuestra Comision a una Persona de mi confianza q^e lo revelò a la Corte de Madrid; y ademas el negoc^{te}. a quien se mando habilitarnos revelo todo esto a varias Personas: De modo que quando llegué a Mad^d. ya sabia el Miñro español todo lo que pasaba y hasta el nomb^e. fing^{do}. de Monsr. Northon q^e Yo debia tomar. En Lisboa se hablaba tambien sin recato; por esto resolvi no efectar un incognito que no podia guardar y preferi un pretexto mas sencillo y claro que evitase sospechas fundadas.

No hè dejado de hacer una reflexion reducida a que la España empezo la guerra en distinto tiempo, y con distintos motivos q° la franc^a., por lo q° no era irregular que tambien hiciese la Paz separadam^{te}.; pero a este argum^{to}. se dà la resp^{ta}. de que la Inglaterra quando rehuso los buenos deseos de la mediac^{on}. del Rey Cat^{co}. y continuo sus ofensas contra el territorio y marina de españa, obligo a esta a unirse con la franc^a. y contraher nuevos empeños para hacer esta guerra, por lo q°. es imposible faltar a ellos; y la misma Inglaterra no tendria confianza en los q° aora contragese con la España, si esta fuese capaz de romper-los con facilidad y de faltar a la buena fe de los tratados—

No obtante todas estas dificultades, concibo, que si la Inglaterra hallase el modo de contentar a la España, y de concertar con ella un ajuste decente para la franc^a., podia entonces, si el Ministerio frances no queria acceder a el, esperar que la españa se acomodase por si sola Esto no lo tengo por imposible y en tal caso se abriria con mas facilidad la Puerta a otras negociaciones, las quales fuesen disminuyendo la fuerza de la union entre las cortes de Madrid y Versalles. Este punto es en mi sentir el mas importante para la Inglaterra, y yà que esta no pueda romper de repente aquella union lo q° seria dificil o imposible, puede a lo menos reducirla a terminos que no tenga que temerla. Puede ser que me engañe; pero con tiempo, paciencia y constancia me parece que se puede adelantar mucho.

Si la francia accediese de grado o por necesidad al ajuste que la España le proporcionase, me parece que esta quedaria mui agradeçida a la Inglaterra; y podria separadam^{te}. tantear de algun tratado particular con la misma España, en que se diese principio a una amistad mas estrecha entre las Cortes de Londres, y Madrid que contrapesase o balancease la union de esta con la de Versalles.

Yo no entiendo de Politica, pero me parece que la mejor es la mas simple y la q°. guia por el camino mas llano y mas derecho como tal reputo el de no descartar absolutam^{te}. a la francia de un ajuste, y ganar la confianza de la España paraq°. se disguste con los franceses y aunq° aparte de ellos, si reusan una Paz razonable. En su defecto sera preciso romper la negociacion. Si se lograse en el tratado comun entre las tres Potencias o en el particular con la España pactar una garantia especifica de los dominios q° queden a estas Naziones en qualq^r Parte del Mundo desp^s. de la Paz se veria ya la España comprometida a no empuñar la Espada contra la Inglaterra en los casos en q^e se tratase de acometer a esta y por conseq^{cia}. no podria arrastrar la franc^a. a la España a la execuc^{on}. de otros pactos anteriores de alianza. A esta garantia à alg^{nas}. ventajas reciprocas de comercio, y a otras cosas q^e indicaré despues, podria dirigirse el tratado particular o separado con la españa.

Pero resta ver como podrian ser excluidas las colonias del tratado, si se ha de contar para el con la franc^a. que es el 2°. punto de la dificultad. Por lo que toca a la España, me costa que no esta empeñada todavia con las Colonias, aunq^e., la veo mui proxima a ello, sino lo corta o detiene una pronta negociacion; y asi el Ministerio español por lo que asi toca, podria tratar con la Inglaterra sin comprehender a las colonias. Mas la francia nunca querra dejar este punto pendiente, y a lo menos querra salvar las apariencias, sin lo qual quedaria inutil toda negociac^{on}. porq^e la España rehusaria seguirla, sin ver antes si la fran^a. se negara o nò a proposiciones decentes; y no reputaria la españa por decente proponer a la franc^a. que faltase abiertam^{te}. a sus trat^{dos}. bien o malhechos con las colonias, desacreditando su palabra y buena fè a la vista de todo el Mundo.

Por esta razon, si se hà de negociar es preciso buscar algun medio termino. El medio que aqui se encuentra es que la Inglaterra afirme y ofrezca que se compondrà y ajustara por si sola, con el Congreso o con las Colonias *en terminos que estas no puedan justam^{te}. recomvenir a la franc^a. sobre la observanc^a. de sus tratados.* Con estas expresiones pudiera salvarse todo; porq^e. si la Inglaterra se ajusta recobrando la dependienc^a. no pueden las Colonias q^e lo avran consentido recomvenir a la franc^a., y si se ajustan obteniendo la independ^{cia}. tampoco podran recomvenir y se acen Deudoras de ella a la misma Inglaterra.

En este medio u otro equivalente es menester pensar para cortar la guerra, y salir la corte de Londres con decoro de las circunstancias actuales; pues si pudiese conseguirse asi, dejando las cosas *in statu quo,* simplemente, hasta ver lo que producia despues una negociacion directa y pacifica de la Inglaterra con las Colonias, tendria esta mas facil^{id}. de ajustarse, y menos que temer en qualquier otro rompimiento, una vez que se huviese apart^{do}. la España de los empeños pres^{tes}. A lo menos Yo lo presumo asi, y me parece q^e no me engaño.

En el tercer punto de la cesion de Gibraltar, me parece que todo lo que podremos obtener sera que no se haga mencion de ella en el trat^{do}. de Paz, ni en sus Preliminares; pero el Gavinete español siempre insistira en que se ajuste por un tratado separado dha cesion por via de cambio, o dando alguna recompensa, y querra que uno y otro tratado se haga y firme al mismo tiempo. En el tal tratado separado pudiera incluirse la garantia general entre ambas coronas de sus dominios de Europa y America y aun algunos socorros reciprocos para el caso de imbas^{on}. tambien pudiera intentarse obtener las ventajas de comercio que insinue anteriormente a lo menos hasta donde lleguen las mas particulares de la francia.

Sino se acuerda lo de Gibraltar jamas podra la España ser verd^{ra}. amiga de la Inglaterra, porque siempre suspirara la nac^{on}. española por el recobro; y en toda ocasion favorable de romper serà arrastrado el Ministerio a una guerra; en lugar de q^e quitado aquel obgeto de discordia, todas las proporciones conspiran a esperar mucha union entre dos Naciones que se miran sin rivalidad, lo que no sucede con los mismos franceses.

No me toca dar consejo sobre el partido q^e ayan de tomar sr̃e estos puntos el Cav^{ro}. Cumberland y su corte; pero mi dictamen seria consultar con todas estas especies y las demas q^e parescan conven^{tes}. al Ministerio ingles, afin de que diga lo que quiere que se haga, siguiendo o cortando la negociacion. Paraq^e. el Cav^{ro}. Cumberland se certifiq^{en} por si mismo de la verdad de mis noticias, y pueda informar a su corte, me paracio mui util q^e viniese a Mad^d. con el pretexto de pasar a Italia. Deste modo podra ver y hablar a el Miñro, y despues seguir el pretexto p^{ra}. salir de España o tomar otro p^{ra}. retroceder, si se huv^{re}. de cortar la negociac^{on}. o esperar nuevas ordenes de su Ministerio. Entretanto no parece que ay inconven^{te}. alguno, pues podra, con noticia de q^e el clima de Valenc^a. es tan favorable como el de Italia al restablecim^{to}. a la salud de su fam^{lia}. pedir licenc^a. para pasar alla, y aun efectuarlo, deslumbrando las espias. Solo se debe tener pres^{te}. q^e las resultas de esta Campaña en todo el tp̃o q^e se retarde la negociac^{on}. pueden variarla mucho, y no se me deben entonces imputar las nuevas dificult^{des}. q^e sobrevinieren.

CUMBERLAND'S OFFICIAL ACCOUNT OF HIS MISSION, TO JUNE 27, 1780[1]

Aranjuez 26th June, 1780

N° 3

My Lord

Tho' I relied upon Your Lordship's kind interpretation of my motives for leaving Lisbon, yet it was no inconsiderable anxiety I suffer'd, till my doubts were satisfied upon the points, which Mr. Hussey's letters had not sufficiently explain'd: As it appear'd to me a case, wherein I might use my discretion, and in which the inconveniencies incident to my disappointment bore no proportion to the Good, that might result from my success, I decided for the journey, which I have now perform'd; and I flatter myself your Lordship will see no cause to regrett the step I have taken.

In my Letter (mark'd E) from Badajoz I acquainted your Lordship with the civil reception given me upon entering Spain; I met the same treatment in every place, thro' which I passed; As I had no Servants with me, that were acquainted with the Country, I accepted the kindness of the Governor of Badajoz, and took a messenger of the King's there in waiting, who was of great use to me by the way.

At Talavera de Reina an Express was waiting with a letter from Mr. Hussey; the first sentence of this Letter set my mind at rest, and determined me to proceed to Aranjuez without sending forward to desire a meeting with him on the way; Accordingly I arrived here on Sunday the 18th ins[t] about 5 o'Clock in the morning, having performed the Journey in nine days, notwithstanding the delays of the Portuguese Conveyances and the premature violence of the heat in Spain.

Not a moment was lost by Mr. Hussey upon our meeting in assuring me by the Minister's authority, that no Article touching the cession of Gibraltar or Minorca woud be obtruded, either in the Preliminaries or Final Treaty; that, upon this declaration, he had consented to use the Minister's own words in his letters to your

1 Original in R.O., S.P.F., Series 94, Vol. 209.

Lordship and me, trusting that I shoud comprehend the implications in his memorand^m, and the verbal message he had sent me by his Servant Daly: As soon as the Minister's hour for rising was come, Mr. Hussey went to him and inform'd him of my Arrival; I received a message of such a nature upon his return, as convinc'd me that my readiness in coming upon the letter and Passports had been well received, and the circumstance of bringing my family agreably to the said Passports, which had been projected by the Minister and Mr. Hussey against my intentions, had also made a favorable impression: An Interview was offer'd me for the Evening of the next day, and even that procrastination excus'd on account of my fatigues. Had I not made ready use of my Passports and Relays I have good reason to believe my hesitation woud have prov'd decisive against any Treaty; whereas now I have the satisfaction of seeing many things point to a favorable and friendly issue, and I flatter myself the business, which Mr. Hussey has prepared with equal skill & integrity, will under your Lordship's protection meet it's completion & Success.

Previous to my arrival the Minister had committed his thoughts to writing, and given them to Mr. Hussey, directing him to state them to me as his own Remarks: In this paper, after some observations not worth repeating, *the difficulties Spain is under for a pretext to separate from her Alliance with france* are principally dwelt upon; These difficulties once removed I have reason to believe there woud remain no obstacle to a separate peace, which might not be accommodated to mutual Satisfaction: If Mr. Hussey had stated these Remarks as his own, they coud have merited no other Consideration than as matter of information, but he was too sincere and friendly to attempt such a thing; on the contrary he shew'd me the paper in the Minister's own hand: I was at a loss to account for this mode of proceeding in Count Florida-blanca, but it has been since explained to be a resource fallen upon to prevent giving umbrage to the British Court, or awakening their jealousy upon mention being made of the American revolted Colonies in the suggestion of a pretext for extricating Spain from her Alliance with France.

This Suggestion was to the following purport, viz, "That Great "Britain, ex mero motu and not as the Condition of any Treaty, or "by the mediation of any Power, shoud declare after what manner "she sees best, that, in order to give a proof of her sincere desire to

"stop the further effusion of human blood, & to remove all cause of
"discord, she is willing and ready to give such terms of peace to her
"revolted Colonies, as shall not fail to convince the World of her
"moderation and equity:"—The Minister will not state any thing as
his own proposition, for the reasons abovemention'd; but his meaning, as convey'd to me, is, that if Great Britain will hold forth
Ouvertures to her Colonies for the purpose of removing the occasion of the war, and in case France shall not thereupon withdraw
from her American Alliance, which Spain professes to reprobate,
Spain will avow her treaty with Great Britain, and, availing herself of this pretext of withdrawing from the war, come into terms
for a separate peace.

This, my Lord, is in substance the idea suggested as a Satisfaction to the punctilio of His Catholic Majesty, who, with every ar-
dent disposition to peace, professes such an attachment to his Engagements, that, without a proof in substance as above, I am assur'd
and well inclined to believe he will not be brought into a separate
Accommodation. If I had been authoriz'd to have discuss'd this
point, I coud no doubt have given proofs sufficient of Great Britain's
moderation in the Nomination of Commissioners, their Instructions
and Proceedings; but from this I am debarr'd; I do however conceive that a detail of these Ouvertures and a declaration, that the
same disposition and desire for accommodating with the Colonies
continues, will be the very measure in request; An actual Treaty to
be set on foot with the Colonies cannot be within the meaning of
Spain; That depends not upon the goodwill of one party, but the
Concurrence of both: I am sorry not to be able to write more
explicitly on this point; but the reserve of the Minister, with a
view of not giving umbrage, is such, that neither Mr. Hussey nor
myself can extract more than the above general suggestion, referring
to Great Britain what the specific mode and measure shall be.

The moment for detaching Spain is now as favorable as ever;
She is still upon the worst terms with France: Not only the King
of Naples but the Queen of Portugal has written pressingly to His
Catholic Majesty to make peace with England; A plan having been
given in by the Duc de Crillon for storming Gibraltar, the King's
Confessor has expressly declared, that if such Orders are given,
he will quit the Court: The Duc d'Almodovar upon the expectation
of Peace since my Arrival has solicited a renewal of his Embassy

to London, and his Uncle the Duc de Losada has actually moved the King in his behalf, and by his great influence over the Sovereign becomes an Advocate of much importance; These and many other Circumstances conspire to press the scale for peace—On the opposite side we may place their unretreiv'd disgrace in the relief of Gibraltar, their hopes in the Grand Armament from Cadiz of the 28ᵗʰ of April; their overrated Successes in West Florida, and their belief that your Expeditions to the South American Continent are dropt and that Sir Edwd Hughes's condition disables him from any Enterprize against the Manillas: Of Sir George Rodney and his Actions they think & speak with reverence and dread; The American Minister Mr. Jay they hold at a distance, and have given some harsh answers to the french Ambassador on his account; the bills of Exchange, drawn to a great amount in Jay's favour by the Congress on Spain, have been one and all sent home unpaid.

My Instructions being peremptory against entering into discussion of any Propositions tending to terms of reconciliation between the King and his Colonies, or between Great Britain and France, I form'd my Reply to the paper of Observations in conformity thereto, and in the morning of the 19th Mr. Hussey carried it to the Minister: The said paper containing an avow'd Acquiescence as to the points of Gibraltar and Minorca, I signified my readiness to wait on the Minister according to his appointment, and in the Evening by Mr. Hussey's introduction had the honour of paying him my respects. After the first Civilities I put into his hands your Lordship's Letter, which I desir'd he woud consider "as conveying "in the language of sincerity the mind of a most just and upright "King, who in his Love of peace rejoices to meet similar Sentiments "in the breast of His Catholic Majesty, and who has been gracious- "ly pleas'd to send me to confer with His Excellency, not for my "experience in Negotiation, but as one confidential to the business "in all it's Stages and zealously devoted to conduct it to an issue." As this Visit passed wholly in expression of civility, I shall observe no further to Your Lordship upon it, than that I was perfectly well pleas'd with my reception, and after an hour's stay, appointed the day next but one ensuing for another meeting.

Upon the day following, (viz the 20th) came a circumstantial detail from Count d'Aranda of your Commotions in London; the whole Conversation instantly turn'd upon this news; all the party

against peace circulated the Story in the deepest colours of despair;
On the 21st in the Evening according to appointment I waited on
the Minister; He had told me to expect the attendance of Sigr Don
Bernardo Campo, and, as I understood we were to have put our
Ideas into writing at this Meeting by way of giving them some
shape, I came prepar'd with my papers in my pocket; but the very
first cast of my Eye upon the Minister and his apartmt, without any
materials for business, and without Sigr Campo to assist, convinc'd
me I was to hear more of tumults, than of peace; and so in fact it
proved: I began to think the whole time woud evaporate in nothing
but a circumstantial detail of an infatuated Mob, with an Account,
which woud have been much more terrible to hear, but for the hope
of french Exaggeration: I gave His Excellency's relation no inter-
ruption and very few remarks, except to acknowlege the benevo-
lence of His Catholic Majesty, who he assur'd me was penetrated
with regrett and Sorrow at the news: At last he turned his discourse
to the business of the Meeting; he profest on behalf of his King
a sincere desire to treat with England for a separate peace; he re-
lated to me the Circumstance of the Queen of Portugal's letter
above mention'd, and observ'd, that with respect to terms, he saw
no difficulties in the way of our agreement, "find an Expedient only
to satisfy His Catholic Majesty as to his Engagements with france,
and Spain will make it a salvo for treating separately with G Britain:" With respect to America Spain had to this hour resisted every
idea of a treaty; She woud not attempt to interpose her mediation
between G Britain and her Colonies; the part, that France had
taken, was by no means her part or her principle; His Catholic
Majesty had too much the sentiments of a Sovereign not to disapprove of France's interference, nay it had given him just offence;
Spain neither before nor since her rupture with England had given
her support to the rebellion; It was true, the Minister himself fore-
saw the Storm when it was gathering, and employ'd a confidential
person to reside in America for the purpose of authentic intelligence,
but he pledg'd his honour that no means were us'd for fomenting
the Revolt.—Such was the general turn of the Minister's Conversation; he spoke largely, but without stating any particular proposition for accommodating Spain in her situation with France. On the
day following he signified a desire to me that I woud write my
thoughts to him, and did not disguise from me, that in the particular

Crisis of Affairs in London, he coud wish I woud accommodate him in waiting for the issue; That he hoped woud be favorable and happy and beg'd me to understand he had no view of receding from the Negotiation for which there was every disposition in Him and his Court that I coud desire; he wish'd also I woud put some propositions upon paper as a basis for the treaty.

On the Evening of the day following (viz friday the 23^d) a letter by Express from Count d'Aranda to the Minister gave an Account of the termination to your disturbances by the punishment of seventeen of the Rioters and the imprisonment of Lord George Gordon; It imported also that an indemnification was directed to the Catholics and foreign Ministers, who had suffer'd by the tumult; no information was given me of this happy Event. On Saturday the 24th I wrote the inclosed Letter and Remarks to the Minister according to his own proposal, and it cover'd some propositions merely founded on the basis of the treaty of Paris and entirely within the limitations of my Instructions. My Letter was submitted to the King on Sunday the 25th and that Night, after the Minister came from His Catholic Majesty, I received his Letter to Your Lordship under a flying seal. On Monday the 26th Sigr. Campo call'd on me at my Apartments, and inform'd me by the Minister's authority, that the reason why he declined stating any proposition, was simply and sincerely from the disposition not to give offence to the British Court by any mention of the rebel Colonies, or even of France, who had made common cause with them; That Spain had twice found herself involv'd in war with G Britain from her zeal to mediate in her disputes, and for that reason she woud not offer any Suggestion, that might alarm the jealousy of the British Cabinet; and either draw an angry denial to her proposition, or perhaps occasion my peremptory recall, and so put a period to the treaty, to which it was fear'd the Ministry of G Britain were not so cordially affected, as that of Spain: He concluded by expressing the Minister's hopes that I had been satisfied with my reception, and that I woud not mix any thing acrimonious in my dispatches touching any subject, on which our opinions might have clash'd; but that I woud put every thing in the most favourable colours, that truth and conscience coud admit, in the hope of accomplishing a reconciliation, in which His Catholic Majesty and all Spain concurr'd in wishing me Success.—Your Lordship will readily conceive what my reply to this discourse of

Sigr Campo must have been. The Minister had on Friday Night received an Account from Count d'Aranda of the riots in London being Subsided, and to this hour had not communicated the intelligence to me, which I had casually learnt from Sigr Don Francisco D'Escarano; Sensible that he had been less forward to inform me of a happy Event, than he was of an unhappy one, he took this opportunity of apologizing thro' Sigr Campo, and sent me the original of Count d'Aranda's dispatch to explain to me the reason of his Neglect. To all this I made reply in the civilest terms I coud use, and on Monday Night the 26th at 12 oClock left Aranjuez, after being attended to the door of my Coach by Sigr Campo and others of the Minister's confidential friends with expressions of the greatest politeness and cordiality.

> Madrid, Plazuela de los afligidos.
> Tuesday, 27th of June, 1780.

I now conclude my Letter to Your Lordship from Madrid, where the Court is expected on Saturday next, and from whence I dispatch my Courier. On the Return, which the wisdom of Your Lordship and the rest of His Majesty's Ministers shall make to this Report, depends the issue of the Negotiation. If His Majesty shall be advised to cause some declaration to be made of his gracious disposition towards a reconcilement with his deluded Subjects in rebellion; and if this be communicated from Your Lordship to Count florida-blanca immediately, or mediately by empowering Me to that effect; and if this be done in mild and friendly terms towards Spain, who stipulates nothing, but submits the whole to Great Britain, requesting it only as a Saving for her punctilio, I think I have strong grounds to say her family Compact will no longer hold her from a separate Peace with G Britain: A great event will then take place in Europe, and a signal honour accrue to Your Lordship's administration: Zealously imploring Providence to guide your Councils for the best, I wait this determination with anxious expectation: I have studied to make a faithfull Report, without concealing or aggravating the truth: If the measure is adopted, which leads to pacification, and in consequence thereof you accompany my Instructions with Powers to sign Articles with the Minister of Spain, I beg also to be directed whether you will cede to Spain any and what part of the Country, compris'd within the boundaries of West florida, and upon

what equivalent: for, tho' the Minister has not open'd on this Subject yet, Mr. Hussey tells me it is a condition he has much at heart,
and which will be strongly contended for in the treaty.

I have the honour to be with all possible respect, My Lord,
                    Your Lordship's most obedt
                    and most humble Servt
                          RICHD CUMBERLAND

Earl of Hillsborough
Princ: Secry of State.

(This address is at bottom of first page).

PAPER DELIVERED BY FLORIDABLANCA CONFIDENTIALLY TO
DON TOMAS HUSSEY ON THE NIGHT OF SEPTEMBER 21,
1780, WHEN HE LEFT FOR ENGLAND[1]

Segun los conocimientos y luces que he adquirido en la corte de
Madrid asi en las conferencias que he podido tener con algunos de
los Ministros, como en los discursos hechos con personas instruidas
y informadas del modo de pensar de aquel Gabinete me parece que
las principales dificultades para venir a una negociacion fructuosa
que finalice la guerra son primeramente, salvar los empeños contrahidos con la Francia por el Rey de España; ni jamas havra paz
firme ni solida, sin la cesion, trueque, ô Cambio de la plaza de
Gibraltar. Siempre que se halle un medio para vincer estas dificultades, creo q^e: los demas puntos seran tan faciles de allanar que se
puede dar por hecha la paz.

En quanto à los empeños de España con la Francia he procurado
averiguar quales son: y segun lo que he podido Saber, parece que en
la substancia se reducen a los Generales de procurar cada Aliado
las ventajas del otro, y no hacer la paz sin ponerse de acuerdo, y
comunicarse sus ideas, y negociaciones. Si hai otros puntos creo
que no seran de gran consecuencia ni podran embarazar el Segui-
miento y conclusion de un tratado.

Supuesto este principio aunque la España no tiene tratado alguno
hasta aora con el Congreso, como la Francia en el suio capituló con
los Americanos, que en caso de romper la Corte de Londres la guerra,
reconoceria la Independencia de las Colonias, y no haria la paz
sinque estas fuesen reconocidas tacita ô expresamente, se sigue de

[1] Original in the AHN, *Est.* 4220, *Expdte.* 2. There is a draft in Floridablanca's hand (Document 108), a copy by Campo (Document 129), and a
copy by Hussey (Document 130). The Hussey copy, which went to England,
is the one reproduced here. The Floridablanca draft is preceded by a note
in Campo's hand (Document 127), viz: "Papel q^e entregó S.E. confiden-
cialm^{te} a D^n Tomas Hussey la noche del 21 de Sept^{re} de 1780 quando se
despidió para Inglaterra. Se reduce a lo q^e el mismo Hussey ha de manifestar al Minist^o Ingles como ideas y observac^s suyas; en consecuencia de
no haber hasta ahora adelantado, nada la negoc^{on} de Dn. Ricardo Cumberland."

aqui que la Francia exigira ésta independencia para hacer la paz,
y que la España no pudiendo hacer la suia sin acordarse con la
Francia, se hallará embarazada para seguir una negociacion mientras no se venza ô allane esta dificultad.

Por estos motivos parece que ô se ha de romper la negociacion actual, ô se ha de reconocer la Independencia tacita ô expresamente, ô se
ha de buscar *algun medio termino,* que corte la Guerra, sinque ni la
Francia y la España comparescan inconsiguientes, ni la Inglaterra haga
aquel reconocimiento formal. No me toca elegir entre todos estos ex-
tremos, pero si me corresponde afirmar por mi honor que no hai otros
para salir de este Labirinto. Hacer una paz particular con España,
faltando el Rey Catolico a sus empeños, es imposible atendida la probidad de aquel Monarca; pero no juzgo imposible atraherle a la aceptacion de un medio termino q^e. salve el decoro de la Francia y de la
Inglaterra, y aun à que trabaje paraque sea aceptado por la primera:
ni menos juzgo imposible, si la Inglaterra da gusto al Rey de España,
inclinarle a un Tratado particular de reciproca conveniencia y garantia entre las dos potencias, nos quite un Enemigo en las Guerras
futuras y nos procure un buen Amigo.

Sobre el punto de Gibraltar se ha allanado la Corte de Madrid a
que no se encluia en el Tratado, quedando siempre Abertura para
concluirlo en un articulo secreto y separado. Como Monsr de Cumberland se ha negado absolutamente á hablar, y aun á *oir hablar*
sobre ésta materia á disconfiado enteramente el Ministerio Español
del suceso de la negociacion: y se han empezado varias conferencias
con los disputados del Congreso, que temo vengan à pasar en algun
tratado, y por esto hemos resuelto que yo me Venga informar à ésta
Corte de todo.

Para ello, y paraque el medio termino que se encuentre sea bien
aceptado es absolutamente preciso que de algun modo se ajuste la
Cesion, Venta, trueque ô Cambio de Gibraltar. Por mis papeles
anteriores, y mis explicaciones he dicho y probado que jamas puede
aver amistad Sincera con la España sino se la buelve Gibraltar. La
Paz no sera durable, y el Ministerio de Madrid no puede separarse
del Modo de pensar de SMC^ca: que está mui fuerte en este punto
con toda la Nacion. Las Promesas hechas à la España por los
Reyes pasados de Inglaterra y la Verguenza de aquel borrón la
tienen irritada y tenaz.

En q^{to}: al medio termino se han discurrido y propuesto tantos desde que se entabló la mediacion de la Corte de Madrid en el año proximo pasado hasta aora que no saben aquellos Ministros lo que podia ser agradable en este punto a S.M.B^{ca}: y al Ministerio de Londres, ni si este tomaria qualquier abertura en algun Concepto contrario a la pureza de intenciones del Ministerio Español; como sucedió en dho año. Y asi desea Saber el modo de concertar este punto teniendo presente q^{to}: se ha discurrido en el hasta aora, y ha propuesto la Corte de Madrid Resta que tanbien discurra y proponga de su Parte el Ministerio Ingles.

CORRESPONDENCE BETWEEN HUSSEY AND FLORIDABLANCA
DECEMBER 1780, AND JANUARY 1781[1]

Exmº: Señor
Señor

Despues de una tardanza de casi dos meses, el Conde de Hillsborough me dictó la siguiente respuesta à lo que le avia expuesto de orden de V E tocante à las aberturas pacificas que pasáron entre las dos Cortes.—Despues diré libremente lo que he observado sobre el asunto.

"Que sentió (el Conde de Hillsborough) muchisimo el que se volviese à tocar sobre el punto de Gibraltar aviendo declarado el Gabinete Britᶜᵒ: que el viage de Mʳ. Cumberland a Madrid, avia sido à condicion que no se le nombrase ni Gibraltar, ni las Colonias Inglesas: y que dicho Caballero en su primer despacho à su Corte, declaró aver obtenido del Sʳ. Conde de Floridablanca la promesa, que estos dos puntos no entrarian en la Negociacion. Que mirar la Cesion ô Cambio de Gibraltar como un *sine qua non* de la paz, es en efecto romper la negociacion; y que asi se mandariá desde luego llamar a Cumberland, si la Corte de Londres no estuviera persuadida que los grandes talentos, y amor Patriotico del Conde de Floridablanca le haría retroceder de unos puntos tan opuestos à la Paz, y por consiguiente à los mutuos intereses de ambas Naciones, y que fiandose en ésto se dexa à Cumberland continuar la negociacion.

"Que la Corte de Londres ignora qual es el medio termino, que insinua el Ministro de España, se debria buscar para hacer la paz sinque ni la España ni la Francia parescan inconsequentes en esta Guerra, y si la España encuentre éste medio termino, la Gran Bretaña se persuade que las miras pacificas de aquella Corte le enduciràn à proponerlo, asegurandose de la mas pronta y sincera aceptacion de la parte de la Gran Bretañaˣ.

X
N: B: El medio termino de la dependencia *feodal* &c que me nombró V E no será admitido.

---

[1] Originals in AHN, *Est.* 4220, *Expdte.* 2. Both of Hussey's letters (Documents 131 and 135) are written and signed by himself. Floridablanca's reply of January 3, 1781, is a draft in Campo's hand. Florida-

"Que por lo que toca a la inconsecuencia de la Francia y de España en ésta Guerra la Corte de Londres piensa que no están sobre el mismo pie. La Francia declaró la independencia de las Colonias, y por consiguiente la Guerra contra la G: Bretaña sin el acuerdo de la España. Esta dice no tener ningun Tratado ni alianza hecha con las Colonias, y sus empeños con la Francia en esta Guerra no ser mas que los ordinarios y acostumbrados entre aliados. Que fundado sobre ésto el Gabinete Brit^{co}: espera que las grandes luces del Conde de Floridablanca verán el verdadero interés de su Patria, y quan contrario le es el Continuar la Guerra en alianza con una Potencia que la dejó engañada en la ultima Guerra, y mui probablemente hará lo mismo en ésta"—

Despues de dictarme el Conde de Hillsborough ésta respuesta entrò en mas conversacion sobre el punto de Gibraltar diciendo que el por su parte se alegraria que fuese cedido a España, pero que el no se atrevería de aconsejarlo al Rei, porque si se alborotase la Nacion, podia ser que este Consejo le costaria su Cabeza.

Despues me vi el mismo dia con Lord George Germain, asegurandole que la respuesta que me dictó el Conde de Hillsborough romperia toda negociacion de paz con España, pidiendole se acordase de lo que me dixo tocante a Gibraltar antes de mi primer viage a Madrid. Me replicó que estava todavia en la misma opinion: que pensaba, y piensa aún, que seria util a la Gran Bretaña hacer la paz con España cediendo à ésta, Gibraltar: que otros miembros del Gabinete pensaban lo mismo, ni creia el que el Rei se opondria a ésta cesion, pero que yo no podia ignorar que en Inglaterra un Ministro vé mil cosas sumamente utiles a la Nacion pero que no se atreveria ejecutarlas—que siempre que llegue el tiempo de ceder a Gibraltar es preciso que sea en profunda paz quando un Ministro no depende tanto ni tiene que pedir Subsidios de la Nacion.

Añadio, que aunq^e: huviera mudado de opinion tocante a la cesion de Gibraltar, la Corte de España acabe de darle suficiente motivo para ello: y con esto me leió varios papeles que llevaba Monsr. Laurens, el Presidente del Congreso que aora está preso en la Torre. Estos papeles era notas de quanto pasó entre la España y las Colonias— desde la conversacion del Duque de Grimaldi en Burgos, con Lee,

blanca's to Hussey of January 20, 1781 (Document 134) is in the Minister's own hand, an unsigned draft. Hussey's to Fernan Nuñez (Document 135) is an autograph signed letter.

hasta una carta en cifra de fecha de onze de Junio proximo pasado del Ministro de Francia cerca de las Colonias, a Monsr: de Vergennes, y su duplicado al Embajador de Francia en Madrid. Esta ultima carta contenia una larga relacion de la Negociacion de España con las Colonias tocante a la navegacion *entera* del Rio Misisippi, y la cesion de aquella parte de la Florida que está dentro del Golfo de Mexico hasta las Montanas de Apalachia y la carta dice que no se podrá llevar el Congreso à acordarlo à España. Concluió Lord Germain con asegurar q^e: el Rei de Inglaterra le instaba continuamente sobre las aberturas aora subsistentes con la Corte de Madrid, mostrando los mas vivos deseos de paz con ésta Potencia.

Esto es todo lo esencial que pasó en este asunto, en que V E vé la mui poca, ô ninguna esperanza que hai de la cesion de Gibraltar: y mucho menos de arreglar el punto de las Colonias especialmente aora que tienen esperanza de Sujetarlas. Están interesados en la Continuacion de M^r. Cumberland en Madrid, porque esto entretiene la Nacion Inglesa con la esperanza de paz, y asi procura el Ministerio mas facilmente los subsidios A mi no me toca mas despues de ésta relacion, y el Pliego separado de Notas que envió, que de ofrecerme en todo a las ordenes de V E. Si juzgue V E por conveniente que yo vaia en derechura a Madrid, iré desde luego.

Con este pliego van todas las cartas y otros papeles tocantes la negociacion q^e V E me confió. Va tanbien una para V E, del Conde de Hillsborough sobre el Cange. Pasó la orden de S M B^{ca}: al Almirantazgo, de donde baxó a la mesa de Comisionados que estan destinados para la ejecucion del Cange, y D^n: Matias de Gandasegui queda abilitado para transportar los Prisioneros Españoles à la Patria. Envió dos Pliegos del Conde de Hillsborough para Cumberland, el uno contiene solamente la Gazeta de Londres, y el otro es de pura contestacion, sin decir cosa de substancia, sino que no tiene orden de mandar su regreso, y que atiende à sus primeras instrucciones. Las demas cartas son de los hijos de Cumberland en Londres, y creo no contener cosa particular. Envio la mia abierta paraque el S^r D: Bernardo del Campo la lea antes de enviarla a Cumberland, ô que la Guarde si lo juzga mas prudente.

Mientras aguardo las ordenes de V E me conformaré en todo que me aconseje el Ex^o S^r: Conde de Fernan Nuñez. Lisboa à 28 de Diciembre de 1780

B L Má V E
Su mas rendido Servidor y
Capellan
Thomas Hussey

Em° Sr Conde de Floridablanca

Recibí pocos dias ha la carta de Vm̃ de 28 de Dic^bre en q^e me daba cuenta de su feliz arribo a esa corte desp^s de una cortisima naveg^n desde Falmouth.

Quedo ent^do de todo lo demas q^e Vm̃ me comunica relativam^te a sus encargos, y en el interin q^e se me proporciona contestarle con individ^l debo prevenir a Vm̃ q^e se mantenga ahi bajo de aquellos pretextos ô motivos q^e parescan mas verosimiles sin afectacion: en la intelig^a de q^e si en el intermedio necesitaré[sic] de algun socorro en dinero podra pedirselo a ese Embaj^or Conde de Fernannuñez.[2]

Por lo que Vm me escribe, veo que Milord Hilbourough y su corte estan en el concepto de

(Dando este principio se puede comunicar a Cumberland todo lo demas).

Enterado de la respuesta que Milord Hilbourough previno a Vm.me diese sobre la negociacion de paz, que se pensaba entablar; veo que aquel Ministro y su corte estan en el concepto *de que* no se avia de hablar de Gibraltar, ni de las Colonias en el caso de que Monsr. de cumberland viniese a Madrid. En este punto ay una grande equivocacion, porque de nr̃a parte solo se convino en que no se hablase de Gibraltar en los Preliminares, pero se propuso, que por convencion o tratado separado se avia de arreglar la cesion o cambio de aquella Plaza, y efectuarlo al mismo tiempo que los Preliminares de Paz.

Este ha sido mi lenguage uniforme, añadiendo siempre, que sin tal cesion o cambio es imposible que la Paz sea durable, ni que la amistad destas dos Potencias sea verdadera y solida: Y asi la negativa absoluta de la corte de Londres es para nosotros un desengaño de que la Inglaterra no quiere ser amiga de la España, y de que no lo sera jamas; puesto que spre avra esta Manzana de discordia entre las dos Naciones.

Por lo que mira a las colonias, siempre he dicho que era preciso hallar algun medio que salvase el honor de la francia para con ellas, y el de la España para con la francia: Ya ve Vm.que no es compatible

---

[2] This (Document 132) is an undated draft in Campo's hand. A note associated with it gives its date as Madrid, January 3, 1781.

esta respuesta con el concepto del Ministerio ingles de q° no se avia de hablar de ellas.

Aora insinua Milord Hilbourough que Yo sugiera el medio. Vm. y aun todo el Mundo sabe quantos medios se han sugerido por aca, desde la mediacion del Rey anterior â la guerra y ninguno ha sido aceptado por la Corte de Londres. No extraño esta repugnancia porq° pueden no aver sido adaptables a aquel govierno los medios prop^{tos}. pero me parece extraordinario, que no se aya propuesto algun otro, o explicado alguna modification, o circunstancia con la qual nos acercajemos a un punto de reunion, conque el Rey pudiese comvidar prudentem^{te}. a la francia para el gran bien de la Paz gᷓal. Quando uno se resiste a todos los medios de conciliacion, sin dar alguna idea de los que podrian adaptarle, es lo mismo que decir que no quiere Paz. Vm.està enterado de todos los medios que nos han ocurrido, y que solo deseabamos q° el Ministerio ingles nos ayuda discurrir o para dar mayor perfecc^{on}. y probabilidad a los que se han tocado hasta aora, o para hallar alguno nuevo que tubiese mas consistencia: Y asi sobre este supuesto puede Vm.entrar en materia, para ver, si ay algun Camino que nos conduzca al termino de la Paz, y adelantar la negociacion.

Si no entra en estos modos de pensar el Ministerio ingles, quedara al Rey el consuelo de averse prestado a quanto pudiera imaginarse para cortar los horrores de la guerra, sintiendo en los mas vibo de su corazon no aver hallado el medio de lograr el fin. Y en tal caso ya vé Vm.que sera inutil que demos que hablar al Mundo con la permanencia de un Emisario ingles en esta corte. Por lo mismo desea el Rey que Vm.se restituya a Londres sin perdida de tiempo, y ve si aquel Ministerio se presta a explicaciones mas positivas y especificas; pues nada le agradecera S.M. tanto como el desengaño y la verdad. dhas esper^{zas}. grᷓales p^{ra}. tiempos futuros sobre los puntos controvert^{dos}. y unos elogios q° graciosam^{te}. nos da Milord, ni son del genio del Rey ni Yo los merezco. Lo que Vm.sabe y puede asegurar es que aqui ay sinceridad en nᷓas explicac^{nes} i probidad en cumplir exactam^{te}. nᷓas palabras; deseo verd^{ro} de restablecer la tranquilidad por q^{tos}. medios sean compatible con nᷓo honor; y constancia para defender este a pesar de todos los riesgos. El Pardo 20 de En° Dios g° Vm 1781

S^{or} thomas Husey

Exm⁰ Señor
    Mui Señor mio
    Envio à V E copia de la carta que he escrito à M^r: Cumberland, en
que le digo solamente en terminos generales que hasta aqui no he
recebido pasaportes, y que no puedo tomar paso ninguno hasta tener-
los ô ulteriores ordenes.—
    Envio tanbien una esquela que acabò de recebir de M^r. Walpole
en que dice que despachará el Criado de Mr Cumberland para Madrid
mañana, ô el domingo a lo mas tarde. Como pienso que por éste
Criado pueda M^r. Walpole decir à Mr Cumberland, que deba volver
a Lisboa imediatam^{te}: creo que Conviene al R^l: Servicio que el S^r:
Conde de Floridablanca tenga aviso de esto con anticipacion.
                    Buenos-Ayres
                    Lisboa à 19 de
                    B L M a V E
                        Su reconocido Servidor
                            y Capellan
                                Thomas Hussey
Exm⁰. Sr Conde de Fernan Nuñez &c

VERGENNES'S MEMOIR ON THE CONCLUSION OF A TRUCE WITH
GREAT BRITAIN—FEBRUARY 1781[1]

1781 Février
Mémoire (de Vergennes) sur les modalités d'une
trève à conclure avec la Grande Bretagne.
Minute en partie de Rayneval

fevrier 1781.

La Séparation de l'Amérique Sep^{le}. d'avec Son ancienne métro-
pole, est la cause et l'objet de la guerre actüelle. Le Roi fait depuis
trois ans les plus grands efforts pour consolider cette Séparation; la
Cour de Londres, de Son côté, épuise toutes Ses resources pour ra-
mener Ses anciens Sujets à l'obéissance. Les mêmes motifs animent
ces deux puissances, l'honneur et l'interêt de l'Etat; et ces deux
motifs Sont Si grands, Si impérieux, qu'aucun des deux Souverains
ne Sauroit céder, à moins que les circonstances ne lui fassent la loi.

Cependant les calamités de la guerre doivent avoir un terme: les
puissances qui ont actüellement les armes à la main, Sentent égale-
ment cette verité, et il est à présumer qu'Elles Saisiront avec empressement les expédients qui pourront remplir leurs voeux pour la
paix.

Mais ces expédients ne Sont point faciles à découvrir: La France
a des engagemens aussi Sacrés que légitimes avec les Etats-unis;
ceux-cy veulent maintenir et consolider leur indépendance; Le Roi
d'Espagne entend aquérir au moins Gibraltar; Le Roi d'Angleterre,
de Son Côté, rejette toutes ces prétentions, et Se montre déterminé
à défendre de toutes Ses forces des droits qu'il croit appartenir encore à Sa Couronne. Ce Sont des devoirs, des intérêts, des pretentions
Si opposés qu'il s'agit de concilier. il Sera impossible d'y réussir
Sans des Sacrifices, Sans des modifications quelconques. Mais qui les
fera ces Sacrifices? Quelles Seront ces modifications? C'est à les
indiquer que consiste le noeud de la difficulté. on va tâcher de jetter

[1] Original in the *Archives du Ministère des Affaires Etrangères* (Paris),
Series *Correspondance Politique, Etats-Unis*, Vol. XV, folios 269-278.

quelque Jour Sur cette importante matière: on Se bornera aux objets qui concernent l'Amérique Sep^{le}.

Il faut d'abord poser pour principe: que les américains ont Secoüé légitiment le joug de la Grande Bretagne; que cette puissance a Elle même forcé le Roi de faire cause Commune avec eux, et qu'Elle a de même mis les armes à la main au Roi d'Espagne. il resulte de là que l'Amérique, la france et l'Espagne font une guerre juste et même nécessaire, et que le Roi d'Angleterre fait une guerre manifestement injuste: cette double vérité est trop évidente pour que l'on croye devoir en faire le développement.

Si donc le Roi de la grande-Bretagne fait une guerre injuste, il est responsable de Ses Suites; il doit en Suporter les frais; c'est à lui à faire des Sacrifices pour le retablissement de la paix.

Ce principe préliminaire posé, il convient d'examiner en quoi ces Sacrifices devront consister; ce que la france et l'amerique peuvent raisonnablement exiger; ce que S.M.B. pourra accorder Sans deshonneur et Sans trop blesser Sa dignité.

Le Roi et le Congrès ne forment qu'une Seule et même demande, c'est l'indépendance des treize Etats-unis. Cette indépendance est établie par le fait comme par le droit, et il paroit desormais impossible que tous les efforts de L'ang^{re}. puissent la renverser. Ainsi cette même indépendance doit être la base fondamentale de la future pacification.

Mais le Roi d'ang^{re}. forcé d'abandonner Ses Colonies, aura Sans doute une répugnance invincible à Stipuler cet abandon vis-à-vis de la france; et dans le fait cette démarche seroit infiniment humiliante pour ce Prince. il convient donc de la lui sauver: on le peut Sans aucun inconvénient. Comme le Roi n'a point pris les armes par un vain mouvement de gloire et d'ambition, que Son unique but a été et est encore de poser un terme à l'insultante prépotence de l'ang^{re}—et qu'il croit atteindre ce but en assûrant l'indépendance de l'Amérique, peu doit importer à S.M^{té}. de quelle manière et dans quelle forme cet objet Sera rempli; Elle peut Sans difficulté laisser la cour de Londres S'arranger directement à cet égard avec les Etats-unis.

Ainsi le Roi peut consentir qu'il S'établisse une négociation directe entre le Congrès et le Roi de la Grande-Bretagne, à condition, toutefois, que l'indépendance absolue des Etats-unis Sera la baze de cette négociation, et que cette baze Sera pré-établie par les médiateurs.

Mais il est possible, il est même probable que le Roi d'Ang^{re}. ne voudra point Stipuler d'une manière aussi catégorique et aussi tranchante l'indépendance de ses anciens Sujets; ce P^{ce}, obligé de céder sur le fond, voudra au moins Sauver les expressions et le mode. On pourra encore Sans inconvénient Satisfaire S.M.B. Sur ce point. A un traité deffinitif on pourra Substitüer une trêve à Longues années: cette trêve assûrera le possessoir Sans toucher au pétitoire. C'est de cette manière que les Suisses et les Hollandois ont assûré leur Liberté. Par le traité qui établiroit la trêve, Les 13. Etats-unis Seroient regardés comme indépendants de fait; on leur accorderoit et garantiroit la jouissance paisible et illimitée de tous les droits de la Souveraineté, en un mot, on prendroit pour modèle, à quelques points près, la Trêve conclue en 1609. entre l'Espagne et les Provinces-unies.

La Trêve dont il S'agit, loin d'être nuisible à la france, Semble au contraire lui presenter des avantages qui ne resulteroient peut-être pas d'un traité deffinitif. En effet, en terminant Sa querelle avec les Colonies la cour de Londres feroit probablement tout ce qui dépendroit d'Elle pour opérer un raprochement prompt et Sincère entre les deux Nations, et Elle ne tarderoit Sans doute pas à proposer au Congres un traité d'amitié et de commerce. Au lieu que Si l'on ne convient que d'une trêve la méfiance Subsistera entre les deux Etats, et nos raports politiques et mercantils Seront consolidés avant que cette méfiance Soit détruite; les américains, contenus par une crainte Salutaire, Sentiront de plus en plus le prix de l'amitié et de la protection du Roi; ils prendront insensiblement l'habitude de traiter avec les françois, et nos manufactures S'accoutumeront à Se plier au goût et aux desirs des nouveaux consommateurs.

Mais Conviendra-t'il aux Américains de Souscrire à une trêve, et dans ce cas, Sur quel pied conviendra-t'il de l'établir.

Les Américains préféréroient certainement une paix déffinitive à une trêve quelconque, parce qu'ils Se trouveroient Sans inquiétude pour l'avenir, et qu'ils Seroient plus libres de faire les arrangements intérieurs et extérieurs qu'ils Jugeroient convenir à leur Sûreté et à leur intérêt. Mais ces considérations ne sont pas assez importantes pour engager le Congrès à prolonger les horreurs de la guerre: le peuple américain en est fatigué, et il Soupire d'autant plus fortement après la paix, qu'il commence à Sentir le poids des impôts et du service militaire; le Congrès de son côté ne se dissimule point toute l'étendüe de Son discrédit, et il prévoit que Si la guerre Se prolonge,

il court le risque d'être Sans resources pour la soutenir. A ces re-
marques on en ajoutera une qui semble être d'un grand poids. Tant
que la guerre durera, l'amérique Sera exposée aux intrigues de la
Cour de Londres, et le Congrès à la trahison; au lieu que Si la paix
Se retablit Soit définitivement ou Seulement par une trêve, le Congrès
Se trouvera en mesure de consolider Son autorité, et il pourra alléger
les charges qu'il a été forcé de mettre Sur les peuples; ceux-cy
jouiront du fruit de leur indépendance; les Torys eux-mêmes s'em-
presseront d'y participer, et Si, contre toute vraisemblance, à l'expiration de la trêve, la guerre devoit recommencer, le Ministère
anglais ne trouveroit probablement plus un Seul adhérent: tous les
Américains Seroient patriotes par habitude, par Sentiment, ou par
intérêt.

Mais les conditions de la Trêve presentent de graves difficultés:
L'ang^{re}. occupe Penobscott, new-york, la Caroline méridionale et la
Georgie. Stipulera-t'on Simplement le *Statu* quo, ou exigera-t'on que
la Cour de Londres retire une partie ou la totalité des troupes qu'Elle
a Sur le continent de l'Amérique?

Il Suffit de Considérer la position géographique de New-york, pour
Se convaincre des avantages inapréciables que L'ang^{re}. tireroit de la
conservation de cette ville. Située au Centre des Etats de l'Est, elle
Serviroit en même tems de place d'armes et de commerce, et l'on
auroit beau déterminer l'usage que les anglais pourroient en faire, ils
enfreindroient journellement toutes les restrictions, en Se persua-
dant que leur conduite ne ramènera point la guerre. Il importe donc,
et pour la Sûreté des Etats-unis, et pour la tranquilité de la france,
que New-york ne demeure point dans les mains de la Cour de
Londres

La Caroline méridionale et la Georgie étant placés à L'extremité
de la confédération Américaine, il y auroit beaucoup moins d'incon-
vénients à maintenir L'ang^{re}. dans la possession de ces deux provinces: La Georgie n'est encore peuplée et cultivée que foiblement, et
Elle n'a aucun port capable de recevoir des Vaisseaux de Ligne; on
en peut dire autant de la Caroline méridionale; Charles-Town, qui
en est la clef et le chef-lieu, peut être fortifié, mais Sa barre empêche
l'entrée des gros vaisseaux, d'ailleurs la chaleur du climat S'oppose
aux progrès de la population, et ote toute énergie aux habitants. Ainsi
ni Savannah ni Charles-town entre les mains des Anglais, ne Seroient
dangereux ni pour l'Amérique ni pour nos Iles. le seul avantage que

la Cour de Londres en tireroit Seroit de faciliter l'aprovisionnement des possessions qu'Elle a dans les Indes Occidentales.

Mais laissera-t'-on la Caroline entière à la grande Bretagne, ou bornera-t'-on Sa possession aux parties de cette Province qui Se trouvent occupées par Ses troupes? Dans l'ordre naturel des choses, la possession réelle doit Servir de règle lorsque l'on établit l'*uti possidetis*, et l'on ne voit pas pourquoi cette règle ne Seroit point Suivie dans le cas dont il S'agit. Ainsi la justice veut que L'Ang^re ne conserve que les points qu'Elle se trouvera occuper au moment de la signature de la Trêve.

Il est cependant une circonstance qui pourroit obliger à donner plus d'étendüe à cette condition. En proposant la règle dont il vient d'être fait mention, la Cour de Londres voudra peut-être l'appliquer à New-york. Dans ce cas, et Si la trêve devoit dépendre de là, il n'y auroit d'autre parti à prendre que celui de laisser à l'Angleterre toute la Caroline du Sud à titre d'équivalent. Mais ce Sacrifice ne devra être fait qu'à toute extremité, afin que les habitants de la Caroline ne puissent accuser ni la france ni le Congrés de les avoir abandonnés gratuitement.

Mais l'execution du plan qui vient d'être indiqué, présente deux difficultés qui méritent toute l'attention de Sa Majesté: on l'a déjà observé dans le cours de ce Mémoire, les Américains desirent et doivent desirer la paix, ils la regarderont comme mal assurée, ils croiront leur indépendance précaire, chancelante et livrée à la merci des Anglois si l'on Se borne à une Trêve! Tel sera du moins le langage des ignorants et des mal-intentionnés; et le Congrés, dont l'autorité ne pose encore que sur les fondements les plus frêles et les plus incertains, osera-t'il, pourra-t'il impunément mépriser les clameurs qui l'environneront? Les Américains les plus éclairés et les plus zélés, entr'autres le Général Washington, ont été Sondés sur cette importante matière, et tous ont rejetté avec force l'idée d'une simple Trêve. Il est possible que les esprits Soient plus calmes aujourdhui, et que la crainte de prolonger la guerre porte les Américains à des Sacrifices qu'ils croïoient inadmissibles en 1779.

Mais qui leur en fera la proposition? Sera-ce le Roi ou les deux Cours médiatrices? La démarche Seroit bien délicate et bien hazardeuse de la part de Sa M^té.; cependant elle seroit practicable moïennant beaucoup de sagesse et de menagements, si elle pouvoit être isolée; mais elle est malheureusement liée au *Statu quo,* et ce

Statu quo, il paroit impossible que ce soit le Roi qui le propose au Congrés: En effet Sa M^{té}. a garanti l'indépendance des 13. Provinces comprises dans la Confédération Américaine; comment le Roi pourroit-il aujourd'hui non-seulement abandonner, mais même conseiller à cette même Confédération d'abandonner plusieurs de ses membres? On n'a ordinairement recours à des Sacrifices de ce genre que lorsque tout est désespéré; or ni les affaires de l'Amérique ni celles du Roi ne sont encore dans une position asusi crüelle, et celles de l'Angleterre ne prospèrent pas assez pour que l'on doive craindre d'être écrasé par leur fortune et par leur puissance.

On ose donc dire que le Roi manqueroit de délicatesse, qu'il violeroit en quelque sorte ses engagements, qu'il donneroit aux Américains de justes sujets de plainte ou au moins de méfiance, S'il proposoit au Congrès de Signer une Trêve en laissant aux Anglois ce qu'ils possédent Sur le Continent de l'Amérique. Il n'y a donc que les Médiateurs, dégagés de tout lien, qui pourroient faire aux Etats-unis une proposition aussi douloureuse.

Je reviens au projet d'une Trêve. Il est à presumer que la Cour de Londres si elle l'adopte, voudra mettre des restrictions à l'indépendance des Etats-unis; Elle demandera pour baze du Traité les propositions qu'elle avoit faites par Ses Commissaires pacificateurs en 1778; et l'empressement, on peut même dire l'affectation avec laquelle Elle a invoqué la médiation de l'Empereur, donne lieu de penser qu'Elle compte à égard Sur le Suffrage de Sa M^{té}. Impériale. Quoiqu'il en Soit de cette derniere conjoncture, le Roi, pour son propre intérêt autant que pour remplir ses obligations, devra rejetter nettement toute restriction, et cet objet est si important, qu'il vaudra mieux rompre toute négociation que de laisser au Roi d'Angleterre le plus léger raport de Souveraineté avec Ses anciennes Colonies. on croit même qu'il Sera de la dignité du Roi d'en faire la déclaration formelle aux médiateurs préalablement à toute ouverture sur les conditions de la paix. Si, comme il faut le croire, le Roi obtient cette condition préliminaire, il pourra hazarder vis-a-vis du Congrès l'idée d'une Trêve, en taisant toutefois celle du *Statu quo;* et il y a lieu de croire que les Conseils de Sa M^{té}. prévaudront, parce qu'il sera, je pense, possible de faire entendre au Congrès, que le point le plus important pour lui est d'assûrer l'indépendance de l'Amérique n'importe de quelle manière. Quant au *Statu quo,* on pourroit différer à en faire la proposition jusqu'à ce que les plénipotentiaires fussent assemblés, parce qu'alors elle sera l'ouvrage des médiateurs, et il Sera plus facile de l'obtenir que si l'on vouloit y amener le Congrès par une négociation préliminaire: Mais le Roi doit être assuré d'avance que New-york sera restitué, car on le repete, cette restitution doit être une Condition *Sine qua non* de la Trêve et du *Statu quo.*

Reste à déterminer la durée de la Trêve. La Cour de Londres voudra en racourcir le terme, et les Américains l'allonger. Comme la trêve ne Sera qu'un palliatif imaginé uniquement pour Sauver au Roi d'ang^{re}. le désagrement de reconnoître définitivement et explicitement l'indépendance de l'Amérique, il conviendra de lui donner une durée analogue au but que se sont proposé les parties contractantes comme les médiateurs, celui d'assûrer l'indépendance des Américains, et de les mettre en mesure d'en jouir; or cette même indépendance Seroit précaire, et les Américains n'en jouiroient point parce qu'ils Seroient agités par la crainte du renouvellement de la guerre Si la trêve navoit lieu que pour quelques années. Il conviendra donc de lui donner une durée au moins de 20. ans. La france a autant d'intérêt que le Congrès à obtenir ce terme, parce qu'elle sera garante de la liberté des Etats-unis, et qu'il lui importe de n'être point dans le cas d'exercer sa garantie.

Cette garantie est établie par l'art^e. II du Traité du 6. fevrier 1778, et elle est énoncée dans des termes qui ne doivent rien laisser à desirer aux Américains. Comme il est possible néanmoins qu'ils ayent des inquiétudes pour l'avenir Si l'on ne fait qu'une Trêve, il Sera de la justice comme de la bienfaisance du Roi de les tranquiliser; Sa Majesté remplira cet objet en offrant au Congrès de prendre avec lui toutes les mesures éventüelles propres à assurer pour toujours l'état et les possessions des Provinces qui seront maintenües dans l'indépendance; l'Espagne Se déterminera probablement à accéder à cette nouvelle Convention.

En resumant les détails dans lesquels ont [*sic*] vient d'entrer, on y trouve les propositions suivantes:

1°. C'est au Roi d'Angleterre, auteur de la guerre, à faire des Sacrifices pour obtenir la paix.

2°. Le premier des Sacrifices à faire c'est l'indépendance de l'Amérique Septentrionale.

3°. Cette indépendance peut être assurée par un Traité deffinitif ou par une Trêve.

4°. Le Roi d'Angleterre quelle que soit la forme que l'on adopte, pourra traiter directement avec les Américains avec l'intervention des deux Puissances Médiatriees.

5°. La Trêve sera à longues années, comme de 20. 25.30. ans &c. les Etats-unis Seront traités comme indépendants de fait, et il ne Sera mis aucune restriction à l'exercice des droits de Souveraineté.

6°. Il Seroit à désirer que le *Statu quo* pût être évité; mais dans le cas où cela ne Se puisse, il conviendra de le borner à la Caroline Méridionale et à la Georgie, et de Stipuler l'évacuation de New-York.

7°. La proposition de la Trêve ne peut être faite au Congrès par le Roi, si elle doit être liée à celle du *Statu quo*; mais en isolant ces deux propositions Sa M^té. pourra S'engager à porter le Congrès à Souscrire à la Trêve, S'il a l'assûrance Secrete que New-York Sera excepté.

8°. Dans le cas d'une Trêve le Roi proposera aux Américains, S'il en est besoin, une nouvelle Convention dont l'objet Sera de les rassûrer contre les attaques de l'Angleterre après l'expiration de la Trêve.

On croit devoir finir le présent Mémoire par la remarque suivante. C'est par nécessité et non par choix que le Roi fait la guerre à la Grande-Bretagne; Sa M^té. a fait Jusqu'à present les plus grands efforts pour en Soutenir le poids; voudra-t-Elle perdre le fruit de tant de dépenses en cédant sur l'objet principal de la Contestation? un pareil Sacrifice ne pourroit être justifié que par les plus grands revers, et que par l'impossibilité de les reparer. S'il étoit le fruit de la foiblesse ou de l'inconstance il terniroit Sans retour la gloire et la reputation de Sa Ma^té.

Les moïens de L'ang^re. sont prêts a être épuisés; elle est Sans allié, Ses forces Sont inférieures à celles de la Maison de Bourbon: dans cet état des choses on peut demander au Roi d'être magnanime; mais Ses condescendances ne doivent porter atteinte ni à Sa dignité ni à Son intérêt.

INDEX

DATE

HIGHSMITH 45-102

PRINTED IN U.S.A.

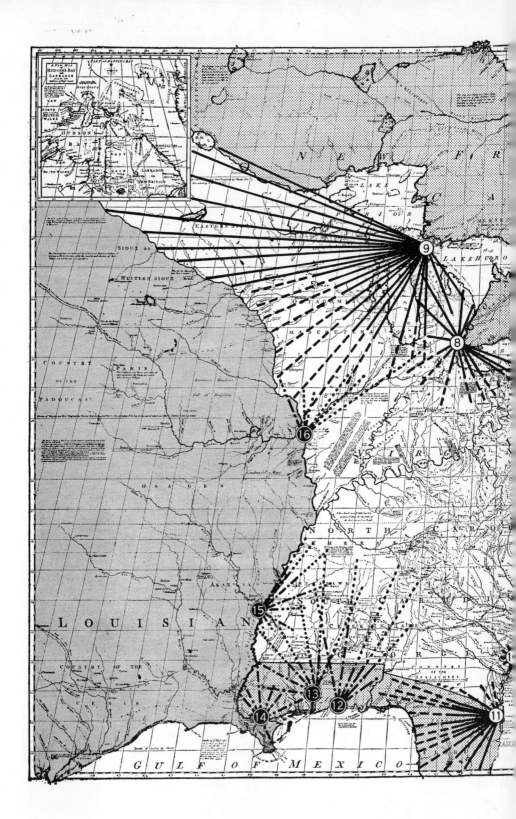